# THE BUSINESS OF
# WATERWAYS
## MANAGEMENT

### A TOE IN THE WATER

# THE BUSINESS OF
# WATERWAYS
# MANAGEMENT

## A TOE IN THE WATER

## LUCIDUS SMITH

authorHOUSE®

AuthorHouse™ UK Ltd.
1663 Liberty Drive
Bloomington, IN 47403  USA
www.authorhouse.co.uk
Phone: 0800.197.4150

Although every care has been taken to ensure the accuracy of the information contained in this book,
no liability can be accepted for any damage, loss or injury caused by the advice or opinion which has
been given or by any errors or omissions in the information which the book contains.

Published by AuthorHouse  08/05/2014

ISBN: 978-1-4969-8840-9 (sc)
ISBN: 978-1-4969-8841-6 (e)

Any people depicted in stock imagery provided by Thinkstock are models,
and such images are being used for illustrative purposes only.
Certain stock imagery © Thinkstock.

This book is printed on acid-free paper.

Because of the dynamic nature of the Internet, any web addresses or links contained in this book may have changed
since publication and may no longer be valid. The views expressed in this work are solely those of the author and do
not necessarily reflect the views of the publisher, and the publisher hereby disclaims any responsibility for them.

## By the same Author

# Contents

# Introduction

The Australian company, Kimberley Environmental Solutions Pty Ltd (KESPL) was formed in June 2006 for the purpose of harvesting water weed in the northern waterways of Western Australia and then turning it into cattle feed.

The proponents of the company were two friends, Len Harris and Neil Woollacott who had come to the realization that there was a serious shortage of cattle feed in the whole of Australia, mainly due to the drought conditions which had existed for several years in the eastern states. This shortage of feed also affected the north of Western Australia (W.A.) where some vast cattle estates were situated along with the main ports in Australia for the export of live cattle to the Middle East, namely Darwin (the Northern Territory), Broome (W.A.) and Wyndham (W.A.) who between them shipped approximately 400,000 head of cattle in the 2004/5 financial year.

During the time that Len Harris had lived in Kununurra, he regularly went water skiing with his family and friends on Lake Kununurra and became aware that the water weed in the lake, which was mainly Ribbon Weed (*vallisneria spiralis*) at that time, was beginning to become a danger and nuisance to everyone who used the lake or lived alongside it. On one such trip, he observed some cattle who had come down to the water's edge to drink from the lake, putting their heads in the water and eating the Ribbon Weed that grew in the shallows.

Initial tests on the Ribbon Weed showed that it was safe and nutritional for cattle to eat so the company was formed to make further investigations regarding the harvesting and processing of water weeds and to prove the viability of a business which could produce such a valuable product out of what had become a serious problem and nuisance.

Two further members were added to the management team, Michael Bray who was an accountant and has since sadly passed away and myself, Alan Smith (I write under the 'pen name' of Lucidus Smith) who was a retired Company Secretary.

A prospectus was produced and circulated and initial investors were found who shared the dream and wholeheartedly supported the environmental intentions of the company. Other people talked about the need to do something to protect the Environment but KESPL management and shareholders were actually 'putting their money where their mouth was', and were trying to do something positive about it for themselves.

The management team soon discovered that there were few books or manuals which dealt with the subject of Waterways Management and little information could be found on the use of water weeds for animal feed, apart from some information about water hyacinth having been fed to pigs in the past. As regards the idea of harvesting water weeds and turning the harvested material into cattle pellets, they were unable to discover anyone else, who had previously attempted to do the same thing.

This book has been written to document all that was learnt during the five or so years that the company existed (it being wound up in 2013) and covers not only our experiences in Kununurra, but the 'Case Histories Section' also looks in detail, at the projects which the Company was invited to bid for, in China and Nigeria.

Most of the major waterways in the world appear to have a weed or algae problem, be it Ribbon Weed in Lake Kununurra, Water Hyacinth in Lagos Harbour (Nigeria), Duckweed in Lake Maracaibo (Venezuela) or Blue/Green Algae in Lake Taihu (China) and sooner or later someone will have to start taking these problems seriously and consider how best to deal with them in a businesslike and efficient long term manner, if the world is to continue to enjoy clean fresh water.

Are Ribbon Weed, Water Hyacinth, Duckweed and Algae terrible problems we have to deal with, or are they an abundant resource we should be harvesting and using?

The author of this book and the other directors of KESPL have all come to the conclusion that they are a valuable resource we should find ways of utilising, so I invite you to read the book for yourself and come to your own conclusion.

Lucidus Smith

## CHAPTER 1

# Original Aims

Kimberley Environmental Solutions Pty Ltd (KESPL) was formed with the aim of proving the viability of harvesting Aquatic Weed and then processing it into animal feed in the form of pellets. The location of the company's operation was to be the Ord River area of Western Australia (W.A.), which included the Ord River Irrigation Channels, Lake Kununurra, Lily Creek Lagoon and possibly Lake Argyle if the initial venture proved to be successful.

Once the idea had been proven, the company would then aim to raise additional capital in order to build a full-scale processing plant to manufacture the feed with the intention of selling the finished product, as stock feed, to the live cattle export market.

It was envisioned that further plants would be built in other areas of Australia where suitable conditions existed.

NOTE.

The Ord River is situated in the north of WA and is a little over three hundred kilometres long and was damned in 1972 to form Lake Argyle (Australia's largest lake) and Lake Kununurra, which are used to supply water for the Ord River Irrigation Scheme (ORIS) Stage 1, which covers approximately one hundred and seventeen square kilometres of farmland.

The original document was entitled 'Business Plan for the Ord River Ribbon Weed Project' and was issued by the proponents in 2006.

The Key Issues as stated in the document are summarized below:

1.  The harvesting of Ribbon Weed has been declared a Controlled Action by Environment Australia, and WH Projects (the original company owned by Len Harris and Neil Woollacott) have been granted the rights as Sole Proponent of such action.

2. Ribbon Weed (*vallisneria spiralis*) is a rhizome, i.e. a grass with subterranean horizontal stems that sends up ribbon-like leaves. It grows to a depth of about 11 meters in the tropics, in large bodies of fresh water.

3. The market for good quality stock feed continues to grow in Australia and globally. Lot feeding in the Kimberley region is firmly established and is steadily expanding. The main restraint to growth is the availability of quality stock feed. Global demand for feed is constant and a good example is the dairy industry in Japan where prices can exceed $600 per tonne.

4. There is a potential market for 100% of the harvestable stock feed from Lake Kununurra, in the local area. The major resource held at this time required to develop, market, sell, and deliver the final product (palletized stock feed), is the classification from Environment Australia of the process as a Controlled Action and we are the Sole Proponent of said action. We have extended this arrangement, with Environment Australia, therefore limiting the possibility of other groups using the same process or material.

5. Response from cattle exporters and cattle growers has been unanimously favourable. Field tests have proven the quality of the product beyond doubt.

6. Three significant points are:

   a. The location is adjacent to established live cattle export facilities (and with 400,000 head of cattle being exported each year, it is estimated that they would consume 96,000 tonnes of food whilst being lot fed in W.A. and a further 19,000 tonnes on their six day journey by sea).

   b. The quality of the feed is expected to be superior to other existing, available products.

   c. The aquatic weed is a renewable resource which is not reliant on weather or climatic variations.

7. The company is seeking Seed Capitalists to fund an initial Feasibility Study to prove the concepts of the business and then a further injection of capital, to fund the setting up and development of a viable business model.

The first meeting for shareholders was held in December 2006 in Mandurah W.A. and approval was given to undertake a Feasibility Study with the following objectives:

- Timeframe – Dec 06 to March 07
- Size Resources
- Meet Local Council & Business People
- Cut Weed, Produce Fodder & Analyze
- Measure Re-Growth & Analyze Water

- Investigate Contracts and Grants
- Obtain EPBC Approvals from DEC
- Plan for Phase Two

The first trip by the new board of directors to Kununurra was undertaken in January 2007 and a further meeting was held for shareholders in February to advise them of what they had found out and to present a new timetable for the year.

A second trip was undertaken in March and a further update meeting held in May when a Mission Statement was presented by the directors and agreed by the shareholders, based on the findings over the previous months.

## Mission Statement for Kimberley Environmental Solutions Pty Ltd

1. To find Safe Solutions for Environmental Problems.
2. To be Solution Innovators when required.
3. To work with Local People, Businesses and Resources.
4. To make our Solutions available Worldwide.
5. To make a Fair Return for our Shareholders and Business Partners.
6. To Initially Focus on these Projects

    - A. Lake Kununurra & Ord River - Aquatic Weed Management
    - B. Ord Irrigation Channels - Harvest Water Weed
    - C. Produce Animal Fodder

NOTE.

Lake Kununurra flows from the dam on the Ord river that created Lake Argyle to the town of Kununurra in the East Kimberley region of Western Australia. The damming of the Ord River was completed in 1972 for the purpose of creating a vast new irrigated farming area. The lake is approximately 52 kilometres long with an average width of 300 to 400 metres.

Lake Kununurra and its associated waterways have been declared a Ramsar Wetland of international significance. As a Ramsar Wetland, all activities on, beneath, or adjacent to the waterway are controlled by Environment Australia (later renamed the Department for Environmental and Conservation (DEC)). The broad aim of the Convention on Wetlands (Ramsar, Iran, 1971) is to halt the worldwide loss of wetlands and to conserve those that remain through wise use and management.

CHAPTER 2

# Overview and Findings

## █ Ord River Area of Kununurra W.A.

The Water Weeds

It was scientifically proven that the most common water weeds found in the Ord River area, i.e. Ribbon Weed, Pond Weed, Cumbungi, Millfoil, Water Lilies and Parra Grass (found on the banks and in shallow waters) were all of nutritional value and safe for animals to eat.

The Harvesting Process

The weeds were not difficult to harvest as such, but trees and submerged objects in Lily Creek Lagoon caused damage to the harvester and the lack of available landing sites meant more time was spent in transporting a load of harvested weed to a landing site than in the actual harvesting process itself.

On the irrigation canals the flow of the water was used to carry the cut weed down to a net which was stretched across the waterway and a conveyor was then used to load it onto a truck, which proved to be an efficient method of removing the weed from the water. Since no 'off the shelf' conveyor was available, the team designed and built their own.

The Drying Process

A satisfactory method for drying the weed was not identified, apart from a conveyor fed microwave oven (sourced from China), which was inspected but never tested in the field by KESPL.

Small quantities of weed were dried by hand in the age old manner used for hay and such like, but the tangled mess of different weeds did not respond well to local mechanized drying methods.

## Business Considerations

In the end KESPL was in business to make a profit for its shareholders, so a decision had to be made as to whether we should continue with the venture, or call a halt while we were still solvent. A list of parameters was drawn up (as under) and a decision made against each, the whole matter then being put before a meeting of shareholders.

| PARAMETER DESCRIPTION | CONCLUSION | |
|---|---|---|
| | GOOD | BAD |
| 1. Is the weed suitable for animals | Yes | |
| 2. Are there any harmful side effects | No | |
| 3. Is there a continuous supply of weed | Yes | |
| 4. Will there be continuing access to the weed (Life of Permit) | | NotCertain |
| 5. Is there a suitable site for operations (landing/processing weed) | | No |
| 6. Have we successfully cut and harvested the weed | Yes | |
| 7. Can it be economically processed | | NotCertain |
| 8. Can we meet all Government and Industry standards | | NotCertain |
| 9. Can we maintain standard/quality of product (NIR Testing) | | Difficult |
| 10. Is there a local market for the product we are able to produce | Yes | |
| 11. Business partners - are they consistent/trustworthy/capable | | ??? |
| 12. Is there ready access to skilled labour | | No |
| 13. Do we have a ready access to finance | | No |
| 14. Are there Serious Risks that are Outside of our control | | Yes |

       Cane Toads
       Harmful farm substances in water
       Obstructions in waterways
       Acrolein from OIC
       Crocodiles/Snakes

## Conclusion

1. That the production of animal feed from naturally grown water plants is NOT a viable business where the management of the waterways is under someone else's control; but the use of the weed for other purposes such as mulch, compost or bio-fuel might well prove to be a viable business.

2. That the production of animal feed from naturally grown water plants is a viable business where the management of the waterways is under the control of the operator and where the area involved is in excess of one thousand acres and is free from obstructions and noxious fauna or flora.

## CHAPTER 3

# Feasibility Study Objectives

The initial Shareholders Meeting held in December 2006 agreed the following:

## ▨ FEASIBILITY STUDY – OBJECTIVES

The Initial Timeframe Set for the study was from December 2006 to March 2007

1. To Size and Document Resources i.e. Area of Water affected, Types of Weed and Infestation rates.
2. To establish best procedures for harvesting and processing aquatic weeds.
3. To test all weeds for suitability as stock feed.
4. To carry out initial re-growth verification tests and establish how the mix of weeds might change after cutting and document any environmental impact that might occur.
5. To analyze the water in different parts of the system and establish local variations and their effect on aquatic weed types and densities.
6. To establish ownership/control/approval processes for all waterways and obtain approval for initial live testing.
7. To meet with local organisations and businesses and investigate opportunities for local partnerships.
8. To confirm economic viability of the project and investigate any grants or subsidies that might be available.
9. Produce a Plan for subsequent Phases of the operation

# OVERVIEW

**Timeframe– Dec 06 to March 07**

Four months proved to be hopelessly inadequate to complete all the various tasks which we needed to do.

These included:

1. The review/analysis/choice/purchase/shipping of suitable equipment.
2. The booking of suitable accommodation and storage facilities in Kununurra.
3. The experimentation and perfection of the various processes we needed to carry out in order to harvest and dry the weed and then turn it into animal feed.
4. The recruitment of local staff and suitable business partners.
5. Obtaining all the requisite permissions we needed to take weed samples and to use the different waterways and landing sites.
6. The analysis of the weed and water and testing the finished product on live animals.

## 1. Size Resources

A waterway is not like a field which a farmer owns and in which he sows his crop and then harvests it. The farmer will know exactly what has happened in that field over many years with regard to what crops have been grown, what animals have used the field, what fertilizers and pesticides have been used there and what weeds, harmful or otherwise, might be found there.

The Feasibility Study concentrated on Lake Kununurra and Lily Creek Lagoon and the Ord Irrigation Channels, with a fleeting look at Lake Argyle.

The Study had to size the area of the waterways that could be harvested and evaluate the volume/weight quality and mix of weed that might be harvested and understand and document the difficulties that would have to be overcome, as well as the exact times of the year when harvesting would be feasible.

Finally it was essential to identify the location of suitable work sites and the transport, power and workforce implications that each required.

## 2. Establish Best Procedures

There is surprisingly little information available about the best way to removed weed from waterways. Some weed grows out from the bank like Cumbungi, some weed is anchored to the bed of the waterway like Ribbon Reed and some weed floats on the water, like Water Hyacinth and some is a mixture of the last two, like Water Lilies.

Apart from the presence of the weed, some of the waterways experienced algal blooms from time to time, which would also need to be collected and either used or disposed of safely.

The study also needed to understand how far beneath the surface of the water the anchored weed needed to be cut in order to avoid fouling the propellers of the boats that used the waterway, whilst at the same time permitting a rate of re-growth that would allow weed harvesting to become a viable business.

## 3. Test for Suitability

The first step was to take samples of the different types of water weeds and have them properly analyzed by a recognized Government Agency.

Next, each individual weed needed to be checked for its suitability as feed for live animals and lastly, a sample of the fodder needed to be produced and tested on live cattle.

## 4. Re-growth Verification

Based on the assumption that different water weeds would grow at different rates to each other and at different times of the year, the Study needed to be able to find and cut sufficient samples of each variety of weed in order to fully understand what the re-growth rates would be and how the mix of weeds at a particular site might change as a result of being harvested.

The Study also needed to understand whether the act of harvesting changed the other flora and fauna found in and around a site and whether that change mattered.

## 5. Analyze the Water

The Study needed to take samples of water at different points in the waterways to understand both the quality and flow of the water at different sites and to document any seasonal variations and uses of different chemicals that might affect our finished product.

## 6. Establish Ownership/Control and Approval Processes

It was essential to have a thorough understanding of who owned and/or controlled the various aspects of the land, water, flora and fauna that we needed to access and what conditions they might wish to place upon us, before we were granted access to them and given permission to proceed.

## 7. Meet Local Council & Business People

We were already aware that there were several Government and Local Agencies whose support we would require, if we were to have a successful long term business based in Kununurra.

The following were the key players we needed to meet and to win over.

| | |
|---|---|
| The Shire of Wyndham and East Kimberley | SWEK |
| The Department of Land | |
| The Department of Water | |
| The Water Corporation | |
| The Department of Environment and Conservation | DEC |
| The Ord Irrigation Cooperative Ltd | OIC |
| Kimberley Development Commission | KDC |
| M & G People | |
| Local key business people - Small Business Centre - Tourism | |

## 8. Confirm Economic Viability

KESPL was a limited liability company with shareholders who one day expected to get a return on their capital, so finding out whether a 'good idea' could actually form the basis of an economically viable business, was something that the directors of the company were mindful of, at every stage of the process.

We needed to understand and document what aspects of the operation could be sub-contracted and which local companies and organisations would be willing and available to assist with this and what that assistance was likely to cost us.

Prior contact with the local Shire had confirmed a willingness to be involved in the Feasibility Study, as had several other local agencies, so a framework for co-operation and the sharing of information needed to be agreed upon and documented.

KESPL had already realised that very generous Government Grants existed to help companies who wished to start up and operate new businesses in Development Regions, like Kununurra, so we needed to understand how these various grants operated and who they were aimed at, as well as what their required in the way of detailed input/commitment from applicants, so a small specialist agency was signed up to help us with this task.

## 9. Plan for Phase Two

Develop and cost a Plan for Phase Two, which would see the creation of a Pilot Plant in Kununurra.

## CHAPTER 4

# Feasibility Study - Problem Areas Discovered

## 1. The Waterways of the Ord River Area of Kununurra W.A.

### Lake Kununurra

The lake was formed in 1963 when the Ord Diversion Dam was built in Kununurra to supply water to the Ord Irrigation Area Stage One, which covered an area of approximately 13,500 Hectares (one hectare = 10,000 sq metres or 2.471 acres).

Although the lake is 55 kilometres (kms) long, some of the last 17 kms after the Spillway from Lake Argyle are not considered safe from a harvesting (boating) point of view, but with an average width of 0.35 kms this still gave us a potential area of approximately 2,000 hectares to harvest.

The lake is known to contain freshwater crocodiles, with the occasional 'salty' making its way there as well, along with over twenty species of fish, including barramundi.

**Cumbungi** (Typha domingensis) a dense bulrush, made large stretches of the shoreline and the lake inaccessible and because of the presence of crocodiles and snakes, made them dangerous places to work in as well. In some instances we found dense mats of cumbungi stretching out from the banks to well over fifty metres into the lake, which made it impossible for anyone without a boat to go fishing in that part of the lake.

**Pond Weed** (Potamogeton tricarinatus) **and Ribbon Weed** (Valisnaria spiralis).

We were shown some areas of the lake where around 95% of the waterway was being chocked by these two weeds. Together they made it impossible for boats to use the lake, since propellers were constantly being fouled and anyone who wished to go swimming or water skiing ran the risk of getting themselves entangled in the weeds, with all the risks that carried.

One landowner we spoke to told us that if he did manage to clear an area around his jetty to launch his boat, very quickly large rotting masses of weed drifted down into the space he had just cleared and chocked it up again.

**NOTE**. We did actually assist this person to clear the water around his jetty and as he had predicted, it was just as bad again a few days later.

## Lily Creek Lagoon

The town of Kununurra sits beside Lily Creek Lagoon which is connected to Lake Kununurra by a narrow channel and covers an area of about one hundred and twenty hectares. Like the lake it is home to a similar group of fish and reptiles, but tends to be a lot shallower than the lake and has dead trees and other obstructions in its waters, which makes boating difficult in some areas.

As the name implies, this area of water was often covered by dense mats of Water Lily leaves which made it very difficult for boat owners to enjoy the facility and with the presence of large stands of Ribbon Weed and the odd crocodile, swimmers had to be constantly on their guard.

**NOTE.** The first time we launched a small boat in Lily Creek Lagoon, I found myself knee deep in the water holding on to the boat's painter, when I suddenly realised that the crocodile who had been basking fifteen metres out in the lake had disappeared, so I made a hasty retreat to the safety of the small jetty.

Much of the far bank of the lagoon was lined with Cumbungi, some clumps stretching out for more than forty metres into the Lagoon and along with the Water Lilies we found dense clumps of Milfoil, which appeared to be prolific in areas where the Lilies had been recently cleared.

## Ord Irrigation Channels

The Ord Irrigation Area Stage One covered approximately 13,500 Hectares and supported a range of crops being grown by over sixty different farmers. With more than 150 kms of main channels and a similar length of drains, which returned the unused water to the Ord River, this controlled area was seen as a real opportunity for KESPL.

Ribbon Weed thrived in the whole canal system, with some Pond Weed growing where the Ribbon Weed had died out, plus occasionally there was a problem with algae.

The drainage ditches were also full of weeds, predominately Milfoil with Para Grass (which had been brought into the area as a cattle food) on the banks and in the shallow water.

Although the Ord Irrigation Co-operative used the poison 'Acrolein' regularly throughout the dry season to try and kill the weeds, they always seemed to return, which is more than could be said for the fish which used to swim in the channels.

## 2. Multiplicity of owners and authorities

During the trip to Kununurra by the directors of KESPL in January 2007 a meeting was arranged at the offices of SWEK where we were able to meet with representatives of the following Organisations, whose support and permission was required in order for us to proceed with the initial Feasibility Study.

Most of the people present were supportive of what KESPL hoped to achieve in Kununurra and said that they would be willing to be involved with our Feasibility Study and wished us luck, but a worrying number suggested that the venture would get bogged down in 'Red Tape' and partisan politics and told of the historical lack of co-operation between the different bodies/organisations in the area, some of whom were present in the room.

### Ord Land and Water Inc. (OLWI).

OLWI is not a regulatory body but a community based land care organization which was formed in 1998 to encourage community participation in the Ord River Irrigation Area.

### Water Corporation.

The Water Corporation is the principal supplier of water, wastewater and drainage services throughout the state of Western Australia. It controls the water from Lake Argyle to the Ord River Irrigation Area and owns the structures like the Kununurra dam and has a say in the quality of the water.

### The Shire of Wyndham and East Kimberley (SWEK)

The Shire of Wyndham and East Kimberley is one of the four local government areas in the Kimberley Region of northern W.A. and covers an area of 45,372 sq miles and has its headquarters in Kununurra.

The shire officials we talked with were always courteous and supportive and were particularly interested in discussing their Lake Vegetation Management Plan, access to Lily Creek Lagoon, and the management of 'Green' waste with us.

### The Department of Lands

This Department advises Government and other agencies on policy, law and practice regarding Crown Land.

We were informed that there existed a 30 metre buffer zone on the banks of the river and the lake which was deemed to be 'Crown Land' and we would need to discuss access across this buffer zone with the Department.

## The Department of Water

This is the government agency that looks after all of W.A.'s water. It manages the availability and the quality of the water in a sustainable way to support growth and development.

It is the owner of Lake Kununurra.

## The Department of the Environment & Conservation (Western Australia) (DEC)

The department had the lead responsibility for protecting and conserving the State's environment on behalf of the people of Western Australia.

Its key responsibilities included broad roles in conserving biodiversity, and protecting, managing, regulating and assessing many aspects of the use of the State's natural resources.

This department was extremely important to KESPL as we discovered that we were not allowed to take weed samples from Lake Kununurra without their written permission and that it would be the DEC who would ultimately allow KESPL to harvest and process water weeds. They had the sign off for all 'Environmental' matters.

## Ord Irrigation Co-operative Ltd (OIC)

Formed in 1996 to operate the water provision and drainage services to the various farms within Stage One of the Ord Irrigation Area, which meant that the OIC serviced seventy one Farmers with a total of 13,500 hectares of land.

We found that a lot of the channels were wide enough for a small boat or pontoon and on average were about two metres deep. The weed problems there had caused them to use Acrolein during the dry season to keep the channels clear of weeds.

They have 150 kilometres of channels and a similar amount of drains and have to flush with chemicals once a month. They used Roundup on weeds when water levels were low.

## Kimberley Development Commission (KDC)

KDC's role is to promote the economic and social development of the region. It was active in the promotion of new industry in Kununurra and was very supportive of KESPL and of the positive environmental and social impact we believed we were going to make to the region.

They awarded KESPL a small grant to assist with the collection of information and the Harvesting Process.

## The Miriuwung Gajerrong People Corporation

As a leading indigenous organisation in the East Kimberley, MG Corporation receives and manages the entitlements and benefits transferred under the Ord Final Agreement to the

Miriuwung and Gajerrong people, the native title holders of their traditional country in the East Kimberley.

We had several meetings with the Miriuwung Gajerrong People Corporation who were **v**ery supportive of what KESPL hoped to achieve, particularly with regard to clearing cumbungi from the shores of Lake Kununurra, as it prevented many of their people from fishing. They told us that water weed was not a problem before the dam was built as each year during the 'Dry Season' the weed largely died out.

## 3. Distance and Complexity affect Timeframe

Kununurra is 3,000 kms from Perth and it takes a day to fly up there and a day to fly back. Most of the times we were there it was hot and humid and everything seemed to take twice as long to do as it did back in the Perth area.

In the end it took nine trips to fully complete the Feasibility Study and to be in a position at the end of October 2007 to apply for a 'Commercial Licence' from the DEC. (see Appendix).

The trips and their various purposes are listed below.

Trip 1 - Mid January 2007 - 5 days - 3 directors
Initial visit - Purpose
To meet people and organizations - visit Lily Creek Lagoon, Ord Irrigation Channels and Drains and take a trip on Lake Kununurra - assess weed problem areas and identify types of weed, quantity and suitability for business purpose.

Trip 2 - Early March - 8 days - 3 directors
Purpose
To re-visit people and organizations - take samples of weeds - try out new cutting equipment on the banks and in the various waterways - make arrangements for a mechanized cut in April.

Trip 3 - Mid April - 5 - days - 1 director and a shareholder (engineer)
Purpose
To Trial new pontoon, Jensen electric cutters and propulsion methods on at least one kilometre of the OIC Channels - examine weed retrieval alternatives - examine partnership options - check re-growth rate of previous cut areas.

Trip 4 - End May - 5 - days -1 director and a shareholder (engineer) and local labour
Purpose
To cut and harvest approximately 3 acres of weed (mainly water lilies) in Lily Creek Lagoon - to trial local indigenous labour - check re-growth rate of previous cut areas - to design a new retrieval system - experiment with drying techniques.

Trip 5 - Early June - 3 days - 1 director and fodder specialist
Purpose
Inspect weeds - determine best method of feed preparation - assess market opportunities for feed - check re-growth and impact of previous cut areas.

Trip 6 - End June/July - 9 - days - 2 directors and 1 assistant and local labour
Purpose
Cut M1 Channel for five kms - test new conveyor retrieval system - dry weed and produce fodder - test fodder on live cattle - check re-growth and impact of previous cut areas.

Trip 7 - End July/August - 9 days - 1 director and 1 assistant and local labour
Purpose
Cut M1 Channel for seven kms - experiment with drying options - check re-growth and impact of previous cut areas - persuade OIC not to inject Acrolein for 1 month.

Trip 8 - End August/September - 9 days - 1 director and 1 assistant and local labour
Purpose
Cut M1 Channel for seven kms - check re-growth and impact of previous cut areas - discuss partnership options with local business groups - persuade OIC not to inject Acrolein for another month.

Trip 9 - End October - 3 days - 1 director
Purpose
Check re-growth and impact of previous cut areas - discuss partnership and funding options with local business groups.

**End of Feasibility Study.**

## CHAPTER 5

# Feasibility Study Results

## 1. Size Resources

### Waterways - Harvestable Areas/Access and Water Weed Quality

1. Lily Creek Lagoon - Estimated by KESPL to have 180 acres of useable waterways.

   The predominant weed was water lily, followed by milfoil and then ribbon weed and pondweed. The weeds were so thick in the lagoon that boat owners were reluctant to use their boats on it.

   We estimated it would yield 2.5 tonnes of dried weed an acre, giving a potential for 450 tonnes if only harvested once a year.

   There were several public slipways that could be used but the number of dead trees and other obstructions dotted around the lagoon would make harvesting slow and dangerous. There were places along the banks where weed could be dumped during the harvesting process and which we were given to understand the shire had used before.

2. Ord Irrigation Channels - Potential for 3 Cuts a year on 72 Kms of navigable channels.

   The predominant weed was ribbon weed with some pondweed growing as well. It grew very thick in some places, but in others (under bridges) it was sometimes absent.

   On trip 6 we cut the weed in 5 Kms of Channels and it yielded around 160 Tonnes of wet weed which amounted to about 20 tonnes of dried weed. Assuming the same level of consistency over the whole distance of the Channels, we estimated it could yield 860 tonnes of dried weeds per annum.

   There were not many slipways from which we could launch a boat into the Channels, so in most cases it would need to be lowered down the bank, which meant that a lightweight pontoon (similar to the one we already had) would be the best solution for that particular problem.

As the water actually flowed along the Channels, we found that the weed floated and could be cut and left to drift into a net which we had strung across the channel. The conveyor system we built was adequate for moving the weed into the back of a truck, but it still meant an operator had to spend a lot of time in the water, guiding the weed to the conveyor.

3.  Lake Kununurra - Estimated by KESPL to have 5,000 acres of useable waterways.

The predominant weed was pondweed with large patches of ribbon weed dotted around and together they covered 95% of the waterway. Cumbungi lined vast areas of the shoreline and stretched out into the water for fifty metres in some places.

We believed there was a potential to harvest the lake three times a year and expected to achieve 2.5 tonnes of dried weed an acre on the first cut, but less on the second and third cuts, giving us a potential yield of around 25,000 tonnes of dried weed a year.

There were many slipways into the lake, but most were privately owned by the farmers who lived beside the lake but everyone we spoke to was so disenchanted with the state of the lake, that we believed permission to use these privately owned slipways would not be a problem. Because of the large stretches of Cumbungi along the shoreline, there were few places where the weed could be dumped onto the banks, assuming we could get permission to do that.

At present dead and decaying waterweeds drift down the lake in huge clumps and eventually end up at the dam where they are lifted out and then dumped. Whilst this was an option for KESPL we decided that we would probably have to design some method of collecting the weed and bundling it up and passing it to a waiting barge which would transport it to a collection/processing site

4.  Lake Argyle - Estimated by KESPL to have 240,000 acres of useable waterways.

We did not carry out a full study of Lake Argyle but on a flight over the lake we did observe large areas of ribbon weed and pondweed in the water.

We estimated that it could easily produce 500,000 tonnes of dried weed a year.

No further study was undertaken/permitted by the DEC.

## 2. Identify suitable Equipment and Establish Best Procedures

The first job was to identify suitable equipment for taking samples and clearing a small area of land or waterway. Whilst ordinary garden tools like shears or secateurs would handle a lot of the requirements, a tool called a 'Y' cutter was purchased from a company in the U.S.A. in order to cut samples of ribbon weed and pondweed which was growing in deeper water. A rope is attached to a pole with a 'Y' cutter attached to the end of it and the pole is simply thrown out into the water and then pulled in and the cut ribbon weed floats to the surface and can be collected by a rake or net.

The knack in handling this tool did not take us long to master, but the cutter was very sharp and the operator had to be careful, especially when cleaning the tool after use, if he did not want to end up with cut fingers.

Suitable equipment for working on the water was not available in Australia so we ended up ordering most of our water based equipment from the U.S.A.

A machine called an Aquatic Vegetation Groomer (AVG) was purchased and could be used by hand or attached to its own floats and pulled along behind a boat. It was found to work well on both soft plants like Ribbon Weed and tough woody plants like Cumbungi and we found it easy to operate both in the water and on dry land, but it only had a small cutting head and therefore was only suitable for taking samples or clearing small stands of weed.

Whilst the AVG worked well for gathering small samples of weed, it was soon realised that we needed something much bigger to tackle the weeds in the M1 Irrigation Canal, where we had been invited by the OIC to run a test on the large stands of Ribbon Weed that existed there.

We purchased a Jenson Lakemower (from Jenson Technologies in the USA - see 'Contacts' in the Appendix) and attached it to the side of a boat and trialled the machine first in Lily Creek Lagoon (where we disturbed a large crocodile) and then in Lake Kununurra. Whilst the single mower worked well, it became obvious very quickly that we would need to operate two, maybe three mowers in the Canals and as soon as we realised that working from a boat did not give a stable enough platform, the team designed and commissioned a small pontoon for use in the Canals, which proved ideal for the purpose.

The picture above shows me cutting stands of cumbungi with the AVG and the picture below shows the first Jenson Lakemower we purchased, with the boat we borrowed during initial trials on Lake Kununurra.

The photograph was taken after we had cleared the water round the jetty of dense mats of both living and decaying weeds. The gadget on the front of the boat was a vain attempt to keep the weeds from fouling the outboard motor.

The picture on the front and back cover of the book, shows the pontoon with two Jenson Lakemowers attached after it had been moored to the bank of the M1 Channel. The pontoon is surrounded by the Ribbon Weed which it had just cut and which had floated down with the current to the net which had been stretched across the channel to catch it.

NOTE.

When KESPL was awarded the contract to clear Lily Creek Lagoon in 2009 a second-hand harvester was acquired (within Australia) and after extensive maintenance and cleaning (to allow movement across state boundaries) it was shipped to Kununurra and worked well for several months on Lily Creek Lagoon.

Some damage was done by the submerged tree stumps and other obstacles and the small carrying capacity meant that more time was spent in travelling back and forward to the bank to dump the weed, than in actually cutting and collecting it.

The above picture shows the purchased harvester working on Lily Creek Lagoon in 2009.

## 3. Test for Suitability

Weed samples were taken of Ribbon Weed, Pondweed and Cumbungi (two samples each) and of Parra Grass, Millfoil and Water Lilies (one sample each).

Independent analysis was carried out by The Chemistry Centre (CC), a government run organisation and by the Agro-Nutritional Research Laboratory (ANRL), a private company and the results, which were all very positive, are shown below.

**FODDER ANALYSIS - KESPL HARVESTED WATER WEEDS**
**SAMPLES DRIED BY The Chemistry Centre (CC) and by the Agro-Nutritional Research Laboratory (ANRL)**
**Note.**
**DB = Dry Basis**
**AR = As Received**

| ID | Description | CC Water %AR | CC Protein %DB | ANRL Crude Protein % | ANRL Digesti-bility % | ANRL MetaEnergy MJ/Kg | CC Crude Fibre %DB | ANRL Acid Detg Fibre % | CC Ash %AR | CC Fat %DB |
|----|-------------|------|------|------|------|------|------|------|------|------|
| A | Ribbon Weed A | 91.7 | 10.5 | | | | 29.2 | | 2.5 | 1.4 |
| H | Ribbon Weed B | 90.2 | 10.6 | 14.2 | 60.6 | 8.3 | 17.6 | 35.1 | 2.2 | 1.6 |
| B | Parra Grass | 50.4 | 7.5 | 9.1 | 49.1 | 6.3 | 31.2 | 46.5 | 8.4 | 1.2 |
| C | Millfoil | 85.9 | 13.1 | 17.7 | 65.4 | 9.1 | 15.5 | 31.0 | 7.3 | 0.7 |
| D | Pondweed A | 79.0 | 9.3 | | | | 23.0 | | 3.8 | 0.8 |
| E | Pondweed B | | | 11.2 | 60 | 8.2 | | 34.2 | | |
| F | Cumbungi A | 75.6 | 5.6 | 5.1 | 42.8 | 5.3 | 37.1 | 52.1 | 3.3 | 2.0 |
| G | Cumbungi B | | | 11.5 | 53.1 | 7.0 | | 42.9 | | |
| I | Water Lilies | | | 10.4 | 57.1 | 7.7 | | 37.4 | | |
| | **For Comparison Purposes - Data from the Internet** | | | | | | | | | |
| | **Cattle Feed Pellets** | | | | | | | | | |
| | Export | | | 12 | | 10 | 33 | | | |
| | Beef | | | 15 | | 11 | 20 | | | |
| | Dairy | | | 16 | | 12 | | | | |
| | **Hay** | | | | | | | | | |
| | Mountain | 18 | | 18 | | | 26 | | | |
| | Ordinary | 15 | | 6 | | 8 | | 38 | | |

# 4. Re-growth Verification and Environmental Impact

All plants re-grew, but some grew a lot faster than others.

There was no determinable change in the flora or fauna of harvested areas, but where the OIC did not use Acrolein for two months in the Irrigation Channels, there was a notable increase in the numbers of fish and other wildlife inhabiting the channels as observed by ourselves and as commented on by others.

### Re-growth Measurements over a Two Month Period

Cumbungi - was the same height as similar Cumbungi that had not been cut.
It actually grew between 15 and 20 centimetres in the first 5 days after cutting.
Even Cumbungi that we thought we had removed completely, managed to grow back to 50% of its original height.

Cut Ribbon Weed - grew back to 50% of its original length (and had fully re-grown within six months).

Pond Weed - grew by only 10 to 15% which was probably the most surprising statistic we found, in view of the way it had completely taken over some areas of Lake Kununurra.

Parra grass - this is an annual crop but new shoots were showing after 5 days.

Water Lillies - little to show after two months but they re-grew as thick as ever the following year

Milfoil - this most certainly re-grew but no actual measurements were taken.

It seemed to take over a large area of Lily Creek Lagoon until the Water Lilly floating leaves re-grew.

## 5. Analyze the Water

Water samples were taken from the following three locations (permission given by the Water Corporation).

A. Lake Argyle - close to the Ord dam

   When full the lake covers just under 1,000 square kms and contains around eleven times the volume of water found in Sydney Harbour.

   We chose to collect the first sample by the Ord dam before it started its journey down Lake Kununurra to ORIS.

B. The start of the M1 Channel.

   The M1 Channel takes water from Lake Kununurra and is situated a short distance from the Kununurra Diversion dam. It is the very first channel in the ORIS system.

C. Lily Creek Lagoon (near the boat shed).

All samples were tested by the W.A. Chemistry Centre and the results were as follows:

| Sample ID | | A | B | C |
|---|---|---|---|---|
| Analyte | Unit | | | |
| Al | mg/L | <0.005 | 0.016 | 0.006 |
| Alkalinity | mg/L | 109 | 58 | 109 |
| Arsenic | mg/L | <0.001 | <0.001 | <0.001 |
| B | mg/L | <0.02 | <0.02 | <0.02 |
| Ba | mg/L | 0.039 | 0.021 | 0.041 |
| CO3 | mg/L | <2 | <2 | <2 |
| Ca | mg/L | 19 | 9.4 | 19.8 |

| | | | | |
|---|---|---|---|---|
| Cd | mg/L | <0.0001 | <0.0001 | <0.0001 |
| Cl | mg/L | 14 | 12 | 13 |
| Co | mg/L | <0.005 | <0.005 | <0.005 |
| Cr | mg/L | <0.001 | <0.001 | <0.001 |
| Cu | mg/L | <0.005 | <0.005 | <0.005 |
| Conductivity | mS/m | 26 | 15.5 | 25.2 |
| Fe | mg/L | 0.009 | 0.18 | 0.012 |
| HCO3 | mg/L | 133 | 71 | 133 |
| Hardness | mg/L | 85 | 44 | 84 |
| K | mg/L | 2.5 | 2.1 | 2.6 |
| Mg | mg/L | 9.2 | 5 | 8.5 |
| Mn | mg/L | <0.001 | 0.006 | 0.004 |
| Mo | mg/L | <0.001 | <0.001 | <0.001 |
| N_NO3 | mg/L | <0.01 | <0.01 | <0.01 |
| Na | mg/L | 19.6 | 14.2 | 17.7 |
| Ni | mg/L | <0.001 | <0.001 | <0.001 |
| P | mg/L | <0.1 | <0.1 | <0.1 |
| Pb | mg/L | <0.0001 | <0.0001 | <0.0001 |
| SO4_S | mg/L | 5.8 | 3.6 | 4.5 |
| Total soluble salts | mg/L | 140 | 85 | 140 |
| V | mg/L | 0.009 | <0.005 | <0.005 |
| Zn | mg/L | <0.005 | 0.011 | 0.007 |
| pH | | 7.2 | 6.6 | 7 |

The very small changes between Lake Argyle (Sample A) and Lily Creek Lagoon (Sample C), shows that over its journey from point A to point C, a distance of almost 60 kms, that the water quality had remained fairly constant.

## 6. Establish the Ownership/Control of the Waterways and the adjacent Land and to understand what the Approval Process is to obtain access and to carry out testing

### Water and Land Access and Operations

The Department of Land (Crown land).
The 30 metre buffer zone on the banks of the river and lake is deemed to be Crown Land and any access/usage must be agreed and authorised by the Department of Land.

The shire (SEWK) could grant access to Lily Creek Lagoon and Lake Kununurra, but everything else that we might want to do was governed by the DEC.

The Department of the Environment & Conservation (DEC) informed us that all matters relating to the environment and the flora and fauna of any area we wished to work in was their responsibility and would be under their authorisation and control.

Anything we wished to do in the form of cutting and harvesting water weeds would need a 'permit' which they alone could issue. This even meant applying for a permit to take samples of the weeds for analysis, in a waterway which was 95% full of weeds.

An example of the detail required by the DEC to obtain a permit is found in the Appendix under - Application for Permit to Harvest Flora from Lily Creek Lagoon for Commercial Purposes

The OIC had complete control of the channels they looked after and willingly gave their permission for us to take samples from the Channels and to use the Channels to test out our equipment and to harvest and process the weed.

**Work Site Options**

Finding somewhere close to Lake Kununurra where we could establish a permanent site to process the weed, proved to be extremely difficult, however, one of the Indigenous Groups we got to know, whose community was close to Lake Kununurra was both enthusiastic and supportive of what KESPL hoped to do and were willing to discuss the use of some of their land and facilities in the early stages of our operation.

It was believed we would require a minimum of five acres of land for storage and processing purposes. It would also need to have a reliable electrical supply.

In the short term, temporary storage of equipment was arranged with a local 'farm machinery' supplier we knew.

## 7. Meet Local Council & Business People and identify Key Players we would need to work with

The first two trips enabled the directors to meet over a dozen different groups and organisations whose guidance/support/permission were needed to proceed with the Feasibility Study. Many gave their support at the initial meeting and just asked to be kept informed as to how things were going.

The Shire of Wyndham and East Kimberley (SWEK) were particularly interested in helping/advising/monitoring the Feasibility Study as were the Kimberley Development Commission (KDC), The Ord Irrigation Co-operative Ltd (OIC) and various Indigenous groups and organisations.

As mentioned above the DEC were in the driving seat with regard to what KESPL would be allowed to do in Lily Creek Lagoon and Lake Kununurra and would be dictating, where and when we would be allowed to do it and what limitations/restrictions we would have to work under.

One thing that did become obvious to us was that many in Government were so fearful of saying 'yes' to us and being responsible for an 'environmental disaster' and ruining their careers, that they would find it much easier to say 'no' or to make us jump through so many hoops that we eventually became tired and frustrated and went away and left them in peace.

On the other hand, we met some very genuine, dedicated professional people, who welcomed us into their community and gave us all the help and support that they could. They spent time with us understanding what we hoped to achieve and could see for themselves the possibility of a whole new industry, springing up in their area, that would employ many local people and bring benefits to their community.

## 8. Confirm Economic Viability

The Study concluded that we could certainly cut and harvest water weed from the Kununurra waterways and that if it could be dried economically (and several of our engineers had ideas as to how that might be achieved), then the weed could certainly be used as animal feed and possibly be combined with other 'bought in' matter, to produce high quality feed pellets.

Initial discussions with a variety of farmers/growers in the area revealed a whole range of crops that were currently wasted, that could possibly be integrated into the feed.

The small amounts of weed (mainly ribbon weed) that were dried and fed to cattle were happily eaten by the cows with no harmful side effects.

The directors were sufficiently optimistic to suggest to the shareholders that the project should move to a second Phase.

## 9. Plan for Phase Two and its Outcome

### 1. To complete DEC requirements for a Commercial License. (See Appendix)

The application was made and a 'limited' commercial licence to harvest weed in Lily Creek Lagoon was issued. Whilst we wanted a licence for Lake Kununurra, this was the best we could arrange at the time, but without receiving a satisfactory payment to cover the costs of harvesting, we realised that this would simply be a very expensive exercise.

### 2. To obtain or to design and build a prototype harvester and processing plant.

The company investigated various harvesters in particular the AquaTractor in the UK and the various models available from Aquarius Systems in the USA and decided that there was no need to design our own harvester for Kununurra.

In conjunction with our feed expert contact, our engineers designed and itemised a pilot processing plant for turning dried water weed, into animal feed pellets (as per item 3. below).

**NOTE.** When KESPL was awarded the contract to clear Lily Creek Lagoon in 2009 a second-hand harvester was acquired (within Australia) and after extensive maintenance and cleaning (to allow movement across state boundaries) it was shipped to Kununurra and worked well for several months on Lily Creek Lagoon.

Unfortunately we were once again unable to dry the weed fast enough and in the end had to dump it. Although we were paid a realistic fee for the work, the harvester was damaged by the various underwater obstacles and the company lost money on the venture.

**3. To travel to China to visit manufacturers of processing plant and to Japan to investigate potential markets for our product.**

Len Harris made a trip to China in late 2007 to look at equipment for our pilot processing plant from several Chinese manufacturers. Over all, Len was impressed with what he saw and we decided that on a 'value for money' basis, we would be able to purchase everything else that we needed from those same manufacturers.

During the visit he was invited to meet the mayor of Wuxi (a town of over six million people) and to discuss with him the algal bloom problem that was affecting Lake Tai (see Chapter 9 Case Study One), which changed the course of the company's focus for the next twelve months.

Japan was never visited.

**4. To convince the OIC to replace poison with machine harvesting in the Channels.**

The OIC were unwilling to do this as it formed part of their Customer Services Charter (see their 'Asset Management section' on their website).

**5. To form joint ventures.**

An outline for a joint venture was discussed with several Indigenous Groups who were most supportive of what we were aiming to achieve in Kununurra but unfortunately the opportunity did not present itself to implement a joint venture with them.

**6. To raise sufficient capital to carry out the above efficiently and professionally.**

We raised extra capital through both new and existing shareholders and were successful in obtaining a small Government Grant from within the Kununurra district.

We applied for several large Government Grants, but were either unsuccessful or the Grant was withdrawn after we had spent many months of time and effort and cost, in applying for it.

With hindsight, we felt that our limited resources could have better been spent elsewhere.

## CHAPTER 6

# Business Considerations and Conclusions

## Basic Requirements for every New Business

When setting up any new business, it is essential to have all the requisite business skills available, for every aspect of the business which you are setting up. Most new businesses fail because they run out of cash, not because they run out of ideas.

The euphoria of doing something new or different or exciting or environmentally challenging, must not be allowed to cloud your 'business' judgement. If whatever you intend doing cannot create more in the way of income than goes out the door in the way of expenditure, then it will fail!

When using your own or other people's hard earned cash to fund a new business, be sure you have done your homework and understand as best as you can, what the opportunities and their associated risks are, along with the costs of doing business, the permissions and support you will require and the time it will take to obtain them and how long it will be before you start to earn any income, directly from the business.

The following is a list of essentials, based on my own experience as a Company Secretary that you must consider if you are thinking of setting up a business which is of a similar nature to KESPL's.

There are many business manuals on the market that will do this in far more detail than I am attempting here.

## Initial Setup

**Advisors** - Accountants - Lawyers - Bankers - Other Consultants
Who has recommended them?
Where are they based?
What are their fees and how do they charge?

Have they any experience in this type of business?

## Directors

What can they bring to the business in the way of skills, funding, relevant experience or contacts?

What time can they commit to the business and how much will they charge for that time?

## Shareholders

How do you find them and how much do they need to contribute and what skills would be useful to you?

What statutory rules apply to promoting your new company?

How often do you meet with them or update them as to how things are going and what will be the consequences for them if things go wrong and they lose their investment?

## Business Premises

Where does it need to be and what tasks will be carried out there?

What alterations will have to be made to accommodate your business and who will pay for this?

Does anyone involved in the business have somewhere suitable to start with?

If you have to lease premises, what terms have been offered and how much would it cost to get out quickly or stay for longer?

How much space is on offer and can it be increased/decreased if necessary and does it offer 'serviced' accommodation or will you have to sort this out for yourselves?

## Back Office Requirements

Staff

What skills do they need and what is the pay rate for those skills and do you need to offer an incentive to get the right person/people on board?

Do you need to draw up Contracts of Employment and who can help you with this?

Will they need Travel Assistance, be fulltime/part-time and what do you have to provide in the way of holidays - pensions - building access - rest rooms etc.?

Furniture - Desks - chairs - cupboards - safe - workbenches - storage racks

Do you need to buy new furniture or will second-hand suffice?

What 'Health and Safety' rules apply and do any of your potential staff have special requirements?

Equipment - Telephones - Computers - Software - Printers/Copiers - Security Cameras - Stationery - Ledgers - Directories - Clocks - Notice board - Cables - Lighting

Do you need to buy new equipment, in which case can any of it be leased, or will second-hand suffice?

What are the costs of installation?

## Planning Requirements

**The Business Plan** - to cover the first three year period
This should be as detailed as you can make it for the first six months with a weekly Cash Flow analysis.
A slightly lower level of detail is required for the next twelve months, with a monthly Cash Flow Analysis.
A lower level still for the next eighteen months but still with a monthly Cash Flow Analysis.

NOTE.

As a new business, your suppliers may not be willing to offer you any credit facilities, but your non-cash customers will be expecting at least 30 days credit from you, depending on which industry they are in.

It will probably take you the best part of a week to produce an invoice and get it to your customer, so by the time their finance department have drawn a cheque and sent it to you and you have then paid it in and it has been cleared by your bank, a period of 6 to 7 weeks could have passed since you actually completed the work for them. Bank to bank transfers are certainly quicker than this, but not every business uses these, particularly if they have cash flow problems themselves.

Your key to success is to have good Credit Management with realistic credit limits for your customers, along with a balanced Cash Flow. There are various credit agencies who will help you with this, 'for a price'.

**The Waterways Management Plan**

Whether you actually own the waterway yourself or are just a contractor working on it, you need access to the official Waterways Plan and if one does not exist, you need to be influential in creating one - see the Appendix for a Guide to a Waterways Management Plan.

**The Equipment Plan**

What equipment do you need for your business and can it be hired or must it be purchased?

How long will it take to get it to where you need it and what border controls/custom requirements does it have to meet?

What service/maintenance/security does it require before it is sent and after it arrives?

Where will it be stored when in use and where will it be kept when not in use?

Does it have to be moved from one site to another and what equipment do you need to move it and whom do you need to notify?

What training/qualification should the operator have and what backup is in place when the operator is absent from work?

If your planning is detailed and regularly updated and you have built in lots of checks and balances and have regular reviews to measure how you are progressing against the Plan, you might well be successful.

If your planning is poor, then you will probably fail!

## Economic Influences

The best of businesses can fail through no fault of their own, so an understanding of the economic influences which might affect the success of your new business is essential.

In making the decision as to whether we should 'Wind the Company Up' or 'Continue for a bit longer' we asked ourselves the following questions, which we termed:

**Parameters for a successful Waterways Management Business in Kununurra**

1.  Is the weed suitable for cattle and other animals?
2.  Does the weed have any harmful side effects?
3.  Can we obtain a continuous supply of the weed?
4.  Will we be granted continuing access to the weed?
5.  Do we have a suitable site for operations (Landing/processing weed)?
6.  Can the weed be successfully cut and harvested?
7.  Is the whole harvesting/processing business economically viable?
8.  Will the end product meet all Government and Industry standards?
9.  Can we maintain a constant standard and quality of the product?
10. Is there a ready local market for the product we are able to produce?
11. Are our business partners consistent, trustworthy and capable?
12. Is there a ready access of skilled labour?
13. Do we have ready access to expansion/development finance?
14. Are there any major dangers or exposures outside of our control apart from the usual business risks?

## Conclusions in Brief

| PARAMETER DESCRIPTION | CONCLUSION | |
| --- | --- | --- |
| | GOOD | BAD |
| 1. Suitability for cattle and other animals | Yes | |
| 2. Harmful side effects | | No |
| 3. Continuous supply of the weed | Yes | |
| 4. Continuing access to weed (Life of Permit) | Not Certain | |
| 5. Suitable site for operations (Landing/processing weed) | | No |
| 6. Successfully cut and harvested | Yes | |
| 7. Economically processed | | Not Certain |
| 8. Meet all Government and Industry standards | | Not Certain |
| 9. Maintain standard/quality of product (NIR Testing) | | Difficult |
| 10. Local market for the product we are able to produce | Yes | |
| 11. Business partners consistent/trustworthy/capable | | Not Certain |
| 12. Ready access of skilled labour | | No |
| 13. Ready access for finance | | No |
| 14. Serious Risks that are Outside of our control | Yes | |

## Conclusions in Detail

- 1. Is the weed suitable for cattle and other animals?     YES

The tests from the Chemistry Centre and from Agro Nutritional and from the weed we dried and fed to the live cattle of a farmer we knew, led us to believe that the weed was a suitable feed for cattle and other animals.

- 2. Does the weed have any harmful side effects?     NO

All the tests showed that the weed was safe and had no apparent side effects, but we recognised that we would need a controlled trial over a much longer period to be absolutely certain of that.

- 3. Can we obtain a continuous supply of the weed?     YES

All the areas of harvested weed re-grew, albeit at differing rates of growth (just as if we had mowed a lawn) and everyone we spoke to congratulated us on the improvement we had brought to the waterways concerned and hoped that we would be able to continue in the future.

- 4. Will we be granted continuing access to the weed?     NOT CERTAIN

Lily Creek Lagoon was time consuming and difficult to work in and our equipment got damaged on the obstructions in the water, so we needed a Commercial Licence for Lake Kununurra from the DEC to make the venture viable.

We could not be certain that such a licence would be granted in the first place and if granted once, we could not be certain that it would be renewed, even if we had been successful and met all of their criteria.

We were fearful that having set up a processing plant at great expense in Kununurra that the DEC might decide not to grant a licence for a second term.

- 5. Do we have a suitable site for operations (Landing/processing weed)?   NO

Despite the vast areas of unused land around Lake Kununurra, some of which would have been suitable for our operation, no public land was offered to us.

Several private organisations did offer to make land available to KESPL, but it was either too small in area or was too far from the lake and other facilities to be viable.

- 6. Can the weed can be successfully cut and harvested?   YES

All the tests KESPL carried out using both our own pontoon and the purchased harvester, proved that we could successfully cut and harvest the weed.

- 7. Is the whole harvesting/process business economically viable? NOT CERTAIN

The problem of drying the weed was never solved by KESPL. We inspected a prototype conveyor fed microwave dryer in China, which we all believed would do the job, but we never had sufficient funds to buy the dryer and to test it.

We had also been unable to test the various ideas which our engineers had come up with, to collect/bale/pickup/deposit the weed, once it had been cut, so we could not estimate what the true cost of a large operation might be.

- 8. Meet all Government and Industry standards?        NOT CERTAIN

Since we had not been able to produce feed pellets, we had no idea whether we could meet the required industry standards.

Our feed advisor told us that we should be able to meet the standards, provided we could guarantee the consistency and quality of our product (Point 9 below).

- 9. Maintain a constant standard and quality of the product?        DIFFICULT

We came to the conclusion that we would need some sort of NIR (Near Infra Red) Testing equipment, to maintain the standard and quality of our product.

Whilst there were thousands of test results for normal cattle feed available within the industry, we were informed that there were none available for water weeds which meant that we would have to create dozens of test results ourselves in order for such a piece of equipment to work.

The creation of such a database, would be time consuming and expensive (probably $500 a shot) and the whole manufacturing process would require us to hold separate quantities of all the dried weed, in order to create a reliable product. Since the weeds often grew together in the waterways, separating them after harvest was going to be extremely difficult if not impossible.

Our results also suggested that the protein level of the various weeds could vary significantly depending on the season and time since the last cut, just like new and old grass in a field.

Creating an animal feed like hay and a recognised high quality feed pellet, were two completely different propositions and since most of our profit forecasts had been based on producing and selling a high quality pellet at a top price, this problem was deemed to be extremely serious.

- 10. Is there a ready local market for the product we are able to produce?    YES

One of the largest herds of cattle I have ever seen, was found less than thirty kilometres from Kununurra. Despite Cattle Stations often covering a hundred thousand acres or more, we were told by many different people that if we could produce cattle feed from water weed, then we would most definitely be able to sell it for a fair price.

We were also informed that at that time in W.A., most of the feed, particularly for the export of live cattle, was being brought in, at great expense, from the Eastern States!

- 11. Are business partners consistent, trustworthy and capable?    NOT CERTAIN

KESPL experienced several instances of where certain senior individuals who were particularly helpful and supportive towards us initially, moved on to new jobs in other parts of Australia, leaving us to discover that their replacement was the complete opposite.

On one particular occasion we acted on a policy decision by one senior executive and invested time, money and resources into a project, only to find that his replacement held the opposite opinion and we ended up the loser.

On the other hand, certain local organisations and individuals, that we would have been happy to become business partners with, were supportive at the start and remained that way right to the end.

- 12. Ready access to skilled labour?                          NO

KESPL did not believe that the skills required to operate weed harvesters, process the weed into feed, manage the whole back office including marketing, sales and logistics were available in Kununurra and that we would need to recruit these skills from outside the area.

- 13. Ready access to expansion/development finance?      NO

The World Recession came at a bad time for KESPL and whilst many people were extremely interested in what we were doing, it became obvious very early on, that banks, financial institutions and venture capitalists would not be willing to support the company financially, without the directors providing punitive personal guarantees, which we were not willing to consider.

Government Grants seemed to be the obvious source of funding to support our business model and whilst on paper, we appeared to meet the criteria for the grants we applied for; none of the major applications were successful, despite the promise of support from senior members of parliament.

- 14. Major dangers or exposures outside of our control?     YES

The Cane Toad did not stop at the Northern Territories state boundary, but travelled on to inhabit the waters of Kununurra. It is extremely poisonous and has already been responsible for the deaths of many of the animals in Kununurra who have attempted to eat it.

KESPL was fearful that Toad infected weed, might end up poisoning thousands of cattle bringing ruin to their owners and the company.

On another occasion in January 2009 we had to make hasty arrangements to move our equipment to a new location as an infestation of 'Singapore Ants' had damaged the electrical systems of some machinery in the vicinity of where our own equipment was being stored

Another concern we had was that our own success in clearing Lake Kununurra of weeds, could eventually make it 'boating friendly' again, with the result that hundreds of speed boats, houseboats and other vessels would use the lake and create pollution which would affect both the water and the weed that grew in it.

Lastly, the go-ahead had been given for the Ord Stage Two Irrigation Scheme to get underway and we had no way of knowing how that decision might impact the waterways and the company, for good or bad.

## FINAL CONCLUSION

With items 4, 7, 8 and 11 being 'NOT CERTAIN' and items 5, 12 and 13 being a definite 'NO', even before item 14 was taken into consideration, the final conclusion had to be that the project was not viable and should be terminated.

A meeting of shareholders was convened and the decision to 'Wind Up' the Company was made.

CHAPTER 7

# The Business Case

## Initial Opportunity

The Business Plan for the Ord River Ribbon Weed Project as presented to potential shareholders in late 2007 stated the following:

'There is a potential market for 100% of the harvestable stock from Lake Kununurra, which is estimated to be 61,000 tonnes at $335 per tonne, resulting in a gross income of $A20,435,000 pa providing a net profit of $A12,000,000.'

NOTE.

$A335 was the current price at that time for pelletised feed for cattle and within the cost of producing that feed was $A180 per tonne to cover transport costs. The cost of transporting KESPL's feed to Broome, Darwin and Wyndham where the live cattle were being exported from, was estimated to be a maximum of $A60 per tonne.

With around 400,000 cattle a year being exported by boat on a six day voyage, having previously spent 30 days being 'lot' fed, it was estimated that they would consume 115,000 tonnes of cattle feed a year.

After the Feasibility Study, it was concluded that the annual harvest of water weed from Lake Kununurra would be in the area of 25,000 dried tonnes a year, with the possibility of an extra 450 tonnes from Lily Creek Lagoon and 850 tonnes from the Irrigation Channels (double this after Ord Stage Two had been implemented).

Our fodder consultant advised us that we would probably not be able to secure $A335 per tonne for our pellets and that a more likely figure would be $A310.

This meant that the potential income was reduced to 26,300 tonnes at $A310 per tonne i.e. $A8,000,000.

If the only profit we made was the difference in transport costs i.e. $120 a tonne less the difference in revenue of $25 a tonne, then we could expect to make a profit of around $A2,400,000.

However, with the possibility of eventually obtaining permission to harvest weed from Lake Argyle, with its potential of yielding 500,000 dried tonnes pa and the possibility of obtaining waste products from other producers in the area to use in feed production, we realised the business had a potential of producing $A200,000,000 of animal feed a year.

## Conventional Farming versus Aquatic Farming

Our contacts in the farming industry informed us that on average one acre of farm land would produce 2.5 tonnes of fodder which would sell for around $A200 per tonne.

We believed that if our harvested weed was simply dried and sold as fodder then it would fetch a similar figure.

### Conventional Farming

One Acre of land produces 2.5 tonnes of fodder
Giving maximum income of                $500 per acre
Less Cost of 9 kilo of seed                 36
Cost of borrowing $1.5000 for land      75
       Cost of ploughing            5
       Cost of planting             4
                           -------
Profit before cost of harvesting etc.     $380

### Aquatic Farming

One Acre of waterways produces 2.5 tonnes of fodder
Giving maximum income of                $500 per acre
Less Cost of seed                       0
Cost of borrowing for land            0
       Cost of ploughing            0
       Cost of planting             0
                           -------
Profit before cost of harvesting etc.     $500

## Plan for a Pilot Plant to Harvest Lily Creek Lagoon and the Irrigation Channels - 2008

NOTE. An opportunity arrived in late 2008 for KESPL to harvest these areas and the following plan was made, but the opportunity did not materialise at that time because we did not receive the Government Grant we had been bidding for, plus we were unable to arrange the shipment of a second-hand harvester from the USA to Australia. We could not find a shipping agent at that time, who would handle this for us at a sensible price.

| ITEM | TOTAL |
|---|---|
| **CAPITAL SETUP COSTS** | |
| **Harvesting Equipment** | |
| Pontoon/Three Cutters/Outboard Motor | In Place |
| Nets/Hand Tools/Batteries/Conveyor | In Place |
| Second-hand Harvester shipped to site | $95,000 |
| | |
| **Transport** | |
| Ute | In Place |
| Truck | Contractor |
| | |
| **Processing Machinery** | |
| Palletising machine | $50,000 |
| Drive motor | $25,000 |
| Transport of machinery to site | $ 8,000 |
| Hammer Mill/Trommel/Mulcher | $20,000 |
| Microwave (small model from China) | $25,000 |
| Conveyors and bagging | $25,000 |
| Electricity connection | $40,000 |
| Storage Shed | $50,000 |
| Transport modified components from Perth | $10,000 |
| Commissioning | $30,000 |
| Civil works | $25,000 |
| Contingency Allowance | $32,000 |
| | |
| **Office** | |
| Cabin Hire/Phone/Furniture/Catering | $20,000 |
| Toilet/Wash Room/First Aid Facilities | $10,000 |
| | |
| **TOTAL CAPITAL SETUP COST** | **$370,000** |

| ITEM | TOTAL |
|---|---|
| **RUNNING COSTS FOR YEAR** | |
| **LABOUR** | |
| Management | $110,500 |
| Commissioning | $ 9,000 |
| Pelletizer plant operators | $64,000 |
| Harvester Operators | $115,200 |
| Truck Driver | $25,600 |
| Airfares | $18,700 |
| Accommodation | $17,600 |
| Total Labour Costs | $360,600 |
| **OTHER** | |
| Fuel for Harvesters and transport | $ 9,000 |
| Electricity | $ 2,000 |
| Bags | $14,000 |
| Hay for mixing @ $100 per ton | $130,000 |
| Trial Feeds | $14,000 |
| Total Other Costs | $169,000 |
| **TOTAL RUNNING COSTS FOR YEAR** | **$529,600** |

| POTENTIAL INCOME | TOTAL |
|---|---|
| **Harvested Dry Tonnes of Fodder** | |
| From The Channels | 850 |
| From Lily Creek Lagoon | 450 |
| Hay from local source | 1300 |
| Price per tonne of pellets | $310 |
| Income from Sale of 2,600 tonnes of pellets | $806,000 |
| Lily Creek Water Management Fee | $20,000 |
| Private Site clearance fees | $ 5,000 |
| **POTENTIAL INCOME FOR THE YEAR** | **$826,000** |

# General Arrangement

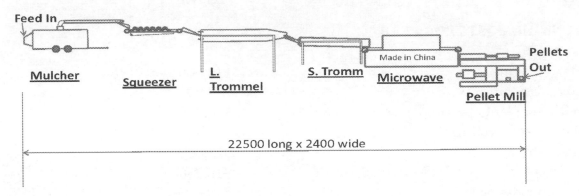

We will need multi level earthworks and 2 trailers to transport

This model demonstrated to us that even on a small scale, we could cover all our costs and be making a good profit by year 3, assuming the Microwave oven was successful in drying the weed.

I should add that no allowance had been made for NIR analysis, which could have increased the Set Up Cost by another $A85,000 for the machine and provision of suitable test results, plus there would be an additional labour cost for the operator.

Our experience in harvesting Lily Creek Lagoon in 2009 under contract to SWEK showed that maintenance and repair of machinery in those difficult waters and the resulting lost harvesting time would also increase our costs and reduce our income.

Although this Pilot Plan was never implemented, various pieces of the Processing Plant were purchased in readiness for when we were able to start operations. Along with second hand hammer mills, trommels and a small power plant, we purchased a brand new Pelletizing machine from China. The microwave oven, however, was never purchased and tested.

## CHAPTER 8

# Business Politics and Negotiations

When we first set out with KESPL we naively believed that because we were trying to do something positive for the environment and we intended to act in an ethical and businesslike way to solve a real and existing problem, that we would be welcomed, assisted, guided and supported in achieving our aims.

In some cases, with some individuals and some organisations, this is exactly what happened, but in other cases it most certainly did not.

Even with hindsight, I am not sure what we should have done differently, as we each had considerable experience, albeit in different fields, in dealing with individuals and organizations both in Government and in the Private sector.

I set out below a few questions, suggestions and pointers, based on our own experiences, that might be of value to others, particularly students, in the future.

## Individuals

Where are people coming from? What is their motivation?

What qualifications and work experience do they have and what private agenda are they working to?

What are their job objectives and what would make them pleased or fearful?

Do they have the power of saying Yes or No and what answer would they normally give? Are they a risk-taker?

Are they an influencer and what is their sphere of influence and how do they achieve it?

Do they have any budgetary or planning control/influence?

How long will this person be in the job and who will influence their successor?

Will their successor take the same or an opposite view?

Does this person like/dislike you or anyone else in the team?

Do you like/dislike this person?

Do you know anyone who can influence this person?

## Organisations

On a scale of 1 to 10, how important is this organisation to you?

What has this organisation said in the past on this subject and why?

Who does it normally align itself with and why?

Who does it normally not get on with and why?

What is its approval process, how long does it take to get a decision and what happens if you do not get its approval?

Is it receiving income or paying any expenses for the matter under discussion?

Do the general public believe it is already OR should be in the future, involved or responsible for solving the problem under discussion?

Which person or department is most likely to support you and who is likely to oppose you? Whose opinion will count most?

Would media or public or individual pressure affect their opinion?

Will you need their support on other issues not relevant to this project?

Will they need your support on other issues?

## The Art of Negotiation

Have an agenda and try to stick to it.

Know what you want to achieve and how you expect to achieve it.

Do not try and achieve too much at the first meeting, you need to appear confident, not desperate.

Agree your required timeframe with the relevant parties within your own organisation.

If you are taking a team of people with you, make sure they all know who is leading the discussion and that they do not speak until the leader invites them to.

Make sure they all understand what the 'cue' is to be quiet.

Understand your own flexibilities and that of the other parties.

What are your parameters for walking away from the table and what are theirs?

What documents will you need to have with you?

What documents should the others have with them?

Are the necessary decision makers present, when considering the level of agreement you need to get from the meeting?

Are there any prior misunderstandings that need to be sorted out?

If you do not know the answer to a question, no matter how embarrassing it might appear, it is better to admit it than to waffle.

If something crops up that you are not expecting, ask for a ten minute adjournment so that you can discuss it with your team.

Mind your language and be polite!!

Do not swear, do not shout, do not be coarse, do not tell jokes (until you know someone really well), do not give away secrets, do not talk about individuals in a personal way AND do not 'chat up' individuals or members of other organisations.

Never 'rubbish' the opposition or talk disparagingly about their products or services or point out where negative feedback may be found.

If the decision has gone against you concede with good grace, so that the door remains open for future opportunities.

CHAPTER 9

# Case Studies in Waterways Management

### ▨ Overview

This section reviews the various Waterways Management problems (mainly outside of Australia) which KESPL were involved with. We never went looking for this work, but in every case, we were contacted and asked to consider whether we would like to propose a solution.

We were never paid for the work we did and were never awarded a contract and in particular, the many months we spent working on a solution for Lake Taihu in China, cost us dearly. Similarly the many weeks we spent designing a working solution for the waterways around Lagos went without any remuneration to the company.

Unless something is done to solve the problems in the world's major waterways, the directors and shareholders of KESPL all believed that an environmental disaster would be unavoidable sometime in the near future, which is why we always got involved.

The first four points on our Mission Statement said it all:

1. To find Safe Solutions for Environmental Problems.
2. To be Solution Innovators when required.
3. To work with Local People, Businesses and Resources.
4. To make our Solutions available Worldwide.

In the hope that a major world organization will decide to take a positive lead in Waterways Management, I am making as much of the detail of each case study available in this Manual as I can piece together in the hope that it might be of some use to someone else at some time.

The Following List gives a few examples of worldwide waterway problems.:

| | |
|---|---|
| • Lake Taihu | Algae |
| • Lake Kununurra | Pond Weed/Ribbon Weed |
| • Lake Maracaibo | Duckweed |
| • Lake Victoria | Water Hyacinth |
| • Lake Wisconsin | Milfoil |
| • Lake Gleason | Pondweed |
| • Queensland Waterways | Cumbungi |

## Case Study One - China – Lake Taihu - Algae

**The Problem**

Lake Taihu or Lake Tai is the third largest freshwater lake in China and covers an area of 240,000 Hectares and has an average depth of two meters. It is located about one hundred and twenty kilometres west of Shanghai and is the water supply for thirty three million people. The main town in the area is Wuxi which is situated on the northern edge of the lake and has a population of more than six million people. Suzhou is near the eastern shore of the lake and it has a population in excess of ten million people.

In the summer of 2007 there was a massive algal bloom of Cyanobacteria, also known as Cyanophyta or blue-green algae, which overwhelmed the waterworks leaving millions of people without drinking water for a week. This particular algae produces toxins that can cause damage to certain organs of the body and to the nervous system. The problem has been well documented and some changes have been made by the Government to solve the problem, in particular, by moving industry away from the area and by removing polluted sludge from the lake and by pumping algae out of the lake.

**Factors Affecting the Solution as we understood them**

Current collection methods were limited.

The main algae disposal method at that time involved dumping the algae into holding ponds which meant that there was a risk that when the algae died, the harmful chemicals might be released back into the waterways, compounding the problem.

NOTE. We were given to understand that small boats with a suction device had been purchased for the collection of the algae and were also told that if all pollution was to cease as from 2007 that the pollutants already in the lake could possibly continue to produce algae for several decades to come.

As I stated in Chapter 5, Len Harris was invited to discuss the Wuxi Algal Bloom whilst on a trip to China and the following solution is the one which our engineers finally arrived at, but negotiations broke down and our solution was never implemented.

**Lake Taihu Information**

| | | |
|---|---|---|
| Total Area of lake | = | 240,000 Hectares |
| Approximate area of lake to be cleared near Wuxi | = | 17,000 Hectares |
| Number of times it must be cleared each year | = | 3 |
| Total Area to be harvested each year | = | 50,000 Hectares |
| Average depth of water | = | 2 Meters |
| Most Common water plant found in lake | = | Water Hyacinth |
| Algae covering most of the lake in 2007 | = | Cyanobacteria |

We first visited Lake Taihu as a team in January 2008 and went for a boat trip on the lake and observed the pollution for ourselves and spoke to local people about the problems it had caused them. These problems included, a bad smell - a cessation of fishing on the lake- restricted movement across lake - a polluted water supply and an adverse effect on tourism.

**Possible Uses for processed Cyanobacteria Algae:**

Compost
Fuel Blocks
Food!!
Bio-diesel (Some researchers believe that an acre of Cyanobacteria Algae could produce 5,000 gallons of diesel per annum.)

**Possible Uses for processed Water Hyacinth:**

Furniture
Rope
Fibreboard
Compost
Fuel Blocks
Animal feed

**The KESPL Solution for Lake Taihu in May 2008**

## SOLUTION OBJECTIOVES

To - Work with the Wuxi Shire to Reduce pollution (especially sewage) and to increase the water volume in order to reduce the nutrient level.
To - Remove Algae and other plant matter from the Northern sector of the lake.
To - Create useful By-products from the Algae.
To - Assist the Wuxi Shire with their Lake Management Plan.

## SOLUTION OVERVIEW

1.  HARVESTERS.
    Clear algae/plants from the lake with 5 x 100 ton capacity Harvesters. These must be capable of travelling at operational speeds of at least 5 k/h and be capable of harvesting 2,000 tons per day and 300,000 tons per season (150 days approx.) Cleared area of water should be kept free from drifting algae and water plants by using a 20kms long 'Barrier Net'.

The Business of Waterways Management

**Concept outline of harvester**

2.  PONTOONS.
    Transport algae/plants from the Harvester to a Pumping Station via a 25 ton capacity Pontoon, travelling at around 12 k/h. Each Harvester will require 4 supporting Pontoons.


NOTE.

- **Capacity to be 25 tonne plus vessel weight**
- **Fabricate from zinc coated mild steel**
    - Pontoons to have fully sealed baffles and may need keels to counteract side wind forces.
    - Operating speed of vessel around 10 – 12 km per hr.
    - Feed and discharge conveyor belt speed around 2 meters per second
    - Central load conveyor belt speed variable and inching capable
    - Sealed spill tray under motor, hydraulic pump, and oil and fuel tanks
    - Operators cabin to be insulated, air conditioned and heated.
    - Completed pontoons need to be transported to Wuxi and off loaded into Lake Tai, therefore may need to be constructed in modular format and assembled on site.
    - Initial contract is expected to be for 20 of these Pontoons

**Transport Pontoons x 20 Off**

3.  PUMPING STATIONS

The algae/weed will be pumped ashore via 5 x 200 tons per hour floating pumping stations. Each must be capable of pumping the algae/plants along 10 kms of pipeline to the shore facility.

4.  OTHER VESSELS.

One main fuel/maintenance vessel capable of carrying 12,000 litres of fuel and travelling at 20 k/h and with pipe laying capacity plus a small maintenance vessel capable of carrying 2,000 litres of fuel.

5.  LOADING JETTY AND MAINTENACE FACILITY.

On shore Loading Jetty and Maintenance facility with 100 metre long maintenance workshop and 3 cranes.

6.  WATER SEPERATION PLANT.

Situated on shore and capable of removing 500 tonnes of water per hour from the algae/plants which arrive via the pipeline.

7.  COMPRESSOR, STORAGE and LOAD-OUT FACILITY

Five compressors capable of processing 120 tonnes per hour each, plus the necessary conveyors to feed into and discharge from the compressors and a storage facility for 2,500 tons, with a load-out facility capable of handling 600 tons per hour.

8.  FERMENTATION TANKS.

Ten Tanks with a diameter of 40 metres and a height of 16 metres (expected to need an area of at least 1.5 hectares per tank which will include item 9 below.) These tanks will receive the compressed algae and allow it to ferment and produce methane gas.

9. METHANE STORAGE TANKS.

Five Tanks with a diameter of 40 metres and a height of 16 metres. Each tank will draw off the methane gas produced by the accompanying two Fermentation Tanks. They will also require a gas compressor to fill the tank efficiently and a boiler to burn some of the gas to create heat/steam to feed back into the Fermentation Tanks and the Residue Treatment Plant

10. RESIDUE TREATMENT PLANT.

What is left in the Fermentation Tanks (probably after 100 days) will be pumped as slurry to filter screens and then on to a settling pond and then to a dryer and compactor where it will be processed into pellets or blocks.

## AREA OF COST FOR SOLVING THE LAKE TAIHU ALGAE PROBLEM

| Item | Description | Notes | Cost in |
|---|---|---|---|
| | | | **Australian $** |
| Harvesters | 5 required each capable of harvesting 2000 tonnes per day | Includes Commissioning by 10 people working 200 hours each per boat | $8,896,000 |
| Barrier Net | 20 kilometre of barrier net | Provisional estimate | $1,500,000 |
| Pipe laying, fuel and maintenance vessel | Capable of carrying 12000 litres of fuel and travelling at 20k/h | Provisional estimate | $1,500,000 |
| Small vessel | | Provisional estimate | $300,000 |
| Pontoons | 20 required capable of carrying 25 tonnes | Includes Commissioning by 5 people working 100 hours each per boat | $16,820,000 |
| Pumping stations | 5 required each capable of pumping 200 tonnes per hour for 10 kilometres | | $14,879,000 |
| Loading Jetty and Maintenance Facility | | Provisional estimate | $8,400,000 |
| Water separation plant | 1 required capable of dewatering 500 tonnes per hour | | $1,572,000 |
| Compressing, Storage and load out facility | 1 system capable of processing 600 tonnes per hour | | $33,825,000 |
| Logistical equipment | 2 x FEL, 2 x dump trucks, 2 x 5t forklifts | Provisional estimate | $1,500,000 |
| Fermentation Tanks | 10 tanks | | $150,750,000 |
| Methane Extraction | 5 Tanks + Compressor + Boilers | | $11,710,000 |
| Residue Treatment | Slurry Pumps, Filter Screens Settling Pond Pipe work Conveyors and Storage | | $13,500,000 |
| | | | $265,152,000 |

These costs do not include manpower costs except where intimated.

## MANPOWER ESTIMATES

### Construction of Vessels and plant.

Management for Project = 112 Man Years
(The majority of which would need to be been spent in China.)

| Running Operation when completed. | TOTAL |
|---|---|
| Harvesters x 5 Vessels x three shifts<br>1 Captain, 1 Mate, 1 Crew (per vessel) | 45 |
| Pontoons x 20 Vessels x three shifts<br>1 Captain, 1 Crew (per vessel) | 120 |
| Fuel/Pipe laying vessel x two shifts<br>1 Captain, 1 Mate, 1 Crew | 6 |
| Small Vessel x two shifts<br>1 Captain, 1 Crew | 4 |
| Pumping Station x 5 x three shifts<br>1 Engineer (per Pump) | 15 |
| Jetty/Maintenance x 3 shifts<br>5 Staff | 15 |
| Water Separation Plant x three shifts<br>2 Staff | 6 |
| Compress/Storage Facility x 3 shifts<br>3 Staff | 9 |
| Fermentation Tanks x 10 x 3 shifts<br>1 Engineer (per tank) | 30 |
| Methane Extraction/Storage/Boilers x 5 Tanks x 3 shifts<br>3 Staff (per tank) | 45 |
| Residue Treatment Facility x 2 Shifts 10 Staff | 20 |
| Office Staff | 48 |
| Management/Board Members | 17 |
| Total Staff Required to Run Operation | 380 |

## Case Study Two – Nigeria – Lagos Waterways
## Water Hyacinth

NOTE. Much of the groundwork used in producing the design for Lake Taihu was also incorporated in our solution for solving Nigeria's Water Hyacinth problems.

### The Problem

To deal with the annual infestation of Water Hyacinth in the rivers and waterways around Lagos each year. In some cases this inhibited transport and seriously affected the fishing industry and other waterway activities.

### Factors Affecting the Solution as we understood them

Water Hyacinth:

It doubles its mass every two weeks by putting out Stolons (runners) which produce new plants.

The flowers produce seed pods with approx 450 seeds in them which can lie dormant at the bottom of a river for twenty years before germinating.

Possible Uses for processed Water Hyacinth:
Furniture, Rope, Fibreboard, Compost, Fuel Blocks, Animal feed, Gas (One Tonne of W.H. can produce enough gas for 40 families.)

Weather information: Seasonal temperatures and rainfall:
Temperature during the day – usually 28 to 30 degree Celsius
Rainfall pattern:
December to April – dry season
April to July – Rainy
August – Break
September to November - Rainy

Hours of daylight = 12 hours (dangerous to work on the waterways outside of daylight hours,)

### Waterway Information

| | | |
|---|---|---|
| Controlling Body | = | NIMASA |
| Area to be cleared | = | 10,000 Hectares |
| Days allocated per annum for harvesting | = | 330 |
| Number of times it must be cleared each year | = | 2 |
| Total Area to be harvested each year | = | 20,000 Hectares |
| Total Area to be harvested each day | = | 60 Hectares |
| Average depth of Water Hyacinth (W.H.) | = | 10 Centimeters |
| Volume of W.H. harvested annually | = | 20,000,000 Cubic Metres |

| | | |
|---|---|---|
| Daily volume of W.H. harvested | = | 60,600 Cubic Metres |
| Average weight of One Cubic Metre of W.H. | = | 60 Kilograms |
| Average weight of daily harvest | = | 3,636 Tonnes |

(NOTE. This volume of W.H. would fill the Centre Court of Wimbledon from the grass court to the top of the roof every five days.)

## SOLUTION OBJECTIOVES

To - Work with the Water Authorities to remove the Water Hyacinth from the waterways and to make them navigable for the whole year.
To - Create useful By-products from the Water Hyacinth

## SOLUTION OVERVIEW

1. HARVESTERS.
Clear Water Hyacinth from the lake with 2 x 35 ton capacity Harvesters.
These must be capable of travelling at operational speeds of at least 5 k/h and be capable of harvesting 1,800 tonnes per day each.

2. TRANSPORT BARGES.
Transport W.H. from the Harvester to the on shore Unloading Station via a 35 ton capacity Barge.
These must be capable of travelling at operational speeds of at least 5 k/h.
Each Harvester will require 3 supporting Barges.

3. UNLOADING STATION
A seven metre wide chute to receive the W.H. from the barges and then a series of conveyors to take the W.H. to a truck loading bay or to a handling facility.

## AREA OF COST FOR SOLVING THE NIGERIAN WATER HYACINTH PROBLEM

| Item | Description | Notes | Cost in US $ |
|------|-------------|-------|--------------|
| Harvesters | 2 required each capable of harvesting 30 Hectares per day | Includes Transport/ Shipping and Commissioning. | $894,000 |
| Transport Barges | 6 required | | $1,530,000 |
| Unloading Station | 1 required | | $1,560,000 |

These costs do not include manpower costs except where intimated.

## MANPOWER ESTIMATES

### Construction of Vessels and plant.

Management for Project = 2 Man Years
(The majority of which would be spent at the shipbuilders.)

| Running Operation when completed. | TOTAL |
|-----------------------------------|-------|
| Harvesters x 2 Vessels x two shifts 1 Captain, 1 Mate, 1 Crew (per vessel) | 12 |
| Pontoons x 6 Vessels x two shifts 1 Captain, 1 Mate, 1 Crew (per vessel) | 36 |
| Unloading Station x two shifts 4 Staff | 8 |
| Office Staff | 5 |
| Management/Board Members | 5 |
| Total Staff Required to Run Operation | 66 |

NOTE. Maintenance and other operations would be out-sourced.

## Alternative Option - Consultancy by KESPL

We did discuss with our contact in Nigeria the option of KESPL staff going to Nigeria and carrying out a study to establish the size and complexity of the problems which W.H. was giving them and to identify and quantify the costs to Government, Industry and Individuals that it was causing.

We would then investigate the options for removing/transporting and storing W.H. and then consider the various alternatives for using the harvested material in an environmentally friendly way.

Although the offer was never formally presented to NIMASA the guidelines we produced for the study are set out below and may be of interest to students.

## Proposal for Consulting Services Regarding Water Hyacinth Control In Nigerian Waterways for NIMASA.

| ITEM | ACTIVITY DESCRIPTION for INFORMATION GATHERING | PLACE | WHEN | TIME IN DAYS | No. OF PEOPLE |
|---|---|---|---|---|---|
| 1 | Establish area of waterway | NIMASA | Before | 0.125 | 1 |
| 2 | Establish seasonal infestation rate | NIMASA | Before | 0.125 | 1 |
| 3 | Establish seasonal growth rate | NIMASA | Before | 0.35 | 1 |
| 4 | List inhibitors and effects | NIMASA | B & D | 0.5 | 1 |
| 5 | Document movement dynamics. | NIMASA | B & D | 0.5 | 1 |
| 6 | Identify Waterway & three different sites on it | NIMASA | Before | 0.5 | 1 |
| 7 | Measure weight & Volume of 1m2 (inc Travel) | Site 1 | During | 0.5 | 1 |
| 8 | Take sample of WH for analysis | Site 1 | During | 0.065 | 1 |
| 9 | Take sample of Water for analysis | Site 1 | During | 0.06 | 1 |
| 10 | Document seasonal variations | Site 1 | During | 0.125 | 1 |
| 11 | Local Information re WH Problems | Site 1 | During | 0.25 | 1 |
| 12 | Measure weight & Volume of 1m2 (inc Travel) | Site 2 | During | 0.5 | 1 |
| 13 | Take sample of WH for analysis | Site 2 | During | 0.065 | 1 |
| 14 | Take sample of Water for analysis | Site 2 | During | 0.06 | 1 |
| 15 | Document seasonal variations | Site 2 | During | 0.125 | 1 |
| 16 | Local Information re WH Problems | Site 2 | During | 0.25 | 1 |
| 17 | Measure weight & Volume of 1m2 (inc Travel) | Site 3 | During | 0.5 | 1 |
| 18 | Take sample of WH for analysis | Site 3 | During | 0.065 | 1 |
| 19 | Take sample of Water for analysis | Site 3 | During | 0.06 | 1 |
| 20 | Document seasonal variations | Site 3 | During | 0.125 | 1 |
| 21 | Local Information re WH Problems | Site 3 | During | 0.25 | 1 |
| 22 | Send all samples for Analysis | Lagos | During | 0.25 | 1 |
| 23 | Identify other plants AND | On Site | During | 0.125 | 3 |
| 24 | Estimate Growth potential if no WH | NIMASA | During | 0.25 | 3 |
| | OBTAIN INFORMATION FOR THE FOLLOWING | | | | |
| 25 | Government costs in dealing with the WH | NIMASA | During | 0.25 | 1 |
| 26 | Shire costs in dealing with the WH | Shire | During | 0.4 | 1 |
| 27 | Industry costs in dealing with the WH | C of C | During | 0.4 | 1 |
| 28 | Individuals costs in dealing with the WH | Local | During | 0.35 | 1 |
| 29 | Days Lost & Cost + Potential for Fishing | C of C | During | 0.25 | 1 |
| 30 | Days Lost & Cost + Potential for Mining | C of C | During | 0.25 | 1 |
| 31 | Days Lost & Cost + Potential for Transport | C of C | During | 0.25 | 1 |
| 32 | Days Lost & Cost + Potential for Tourism | C of C | During | 0.25 | 1 |
| 33 | Days Lost & Cost + Potential for Other Industries | C of C | During | 0.25 | 2 |
| 34 | Document health and safety implications of WH | Dept Health | During | 0.25 | 1 |

| 35 | Estimate the cost to the Health System of WH | Dept Health | During | 0.25 | 2 |
|----|----------------------------------------------|-------------|--------|------|---|
| 36 | Identify suitable site for Process Operations | On Site | During | 0.5 | 3 |
| 37 | Average distance from WH to Process Site | On Site | During | 0.25 | 3 |
| 38 | Decide on removal mechanism | Lagos | During | 0.25 | 3 |
| 39 | Geographical survey for transportation route | On Site | During | 0.5 | 1 |
| 40 | Suitability analysis for transportation options | Lagos/Site | During | 0.5 | 2 |
| 41 | Calculate Storage requirements and options | Lagos/Site | During | 0.5 | 2 |
| 42 | AND Identify potential problems | Lagos/Site | During | 0.375 | 3 |
| 43 | Discuss usage preferences with Government | Lagos | During | 0.375 | 3 |
| 44 | Workforce dynamics + Availability & Cost | Lagos/Oz | During | 0.375 | 3 |
| 45 | Market Opportunities for preferred alternatives | Lagos/Oz | During | 0.375 | 3 |
| 46 | Distribution Options for preferred alternatives | Lagos/Oz | During | 0.5 | 2 |
| 47 | Environmental Impacts of preferred alternatives | Lagos/Oz | During | 0.25 | 3 |
| 49 | Share and Agree all Data Collected | Lagos | During | 0.375 | 3 |
| 50 | Write Presentation for NIMASA | Lagos | During | 0.5 | 3 |
| 51 | Present to NIMASA | Lagos | During | 0.5 | 3 |

|  | Total Elapsed Time for Information gathering |  |  | 15 |  |
|  | Activities Before Trip |  |  | 0.5 | 3 |
| 52 | Receive and Follow Up - Sample Analysis | Oz | After | 1 | 3 |
| 53 | Write Final Report |  | After | 8 | 3 |
| 54 | Travel & Preparation & Medical |  |  |  | 3 |

COST OF CONSULTANCY                                    $72,000

# Report for NIMASA
# Regarding Water Hyacinth Control

| ACTIVITY NUMBER | | INDEX HEADINGS FOR REPORT CONTENTS | TIME IN DAYS |
|---|---|---|---|
| | 1 | Cover Page | 0.125 |
| | 2 | Introduction | 0.125 |
| | 3 | Index | 0.125 |
| | 4 | Investigation Brief and Aims | 1.125 |
| | 5 | Executive Summary | 2 |
| | 6 | Methodology | 1 |
| | 7 | Statistics – Overview | 0.25 |
| A | | Statistics - Sources | 0.25 |
| B | | Statistics - Sizes and Volumes | 0.25 |
| C | | Statistics - Water Hyacinth Dynamics | 0.25 |
| D | | Statistics - Water Hyacinth Analysis | 0.25 |
| E | | Statistics - Costs | 0.25 |
| F | | Statistics - Lost Potential | 0.25 |
| G | | Statistics - Health Implications | 0.25 |
| H | | Statistics - Other Plants | 0.25 |
| I | | Statistics - Workforce | 0.25 |
| | 8 | Findings - Problems – Impacts - Opportunities | 1.125 |
| | 9 | Conclusions and Preferred Solutions | 0.5 |
| A | | End Product - Options & Choice | 0.5 |
| B | | Site - Requirements & Choice | 0.5 |
| C | | Harvesting Options & Choice | 0.5 |
| D | | Transportation Options & Choice | 0.5 |
| E | | Storage Options & Choice | 0.5 |
| F | | Distribution Options & Choice | 0.5 |
| G | | Workforce & Training | 0.375 |
| | 10 | Business Case - Overview | 0.25 |

| | | | |
|---|---|---|---|
| A | | Site - Works & Cost | 0.25 |
| B | | Capital Cost for Collection | 0.25 |
| C | | Capital Cost for Transportation | 0.25 |
| D | | Capital Cost for Storage | 0.25 |
| E | | Capital Cost for Processing | 0.25 |
| F | | Capital Cost for Distribution | 0.25 |
| G | | Running Costs - Overview | 2 |
| H | | Income Potential | 1.5 |
| | 11 | Tender Specifications | 1 |
| | 12 | Government Requirements | 0.5 |
| | 13 | Appendix | 0.75 |
| | 14 | Compile/Check/Re-write & Send | 4.5 |
| | | | |
| | | Total Number of Days | 24 |

# Case Study Three - China – Lake Dianchi
## (or Kunming Lake) - **Algae**

NOTE. Much of the groundwork used in producing the design for Lake Taihu was also incorporated in our solution for solving Lake Dianchi's algae problems.

### The Problem

Lake Dianchi is the largest freshwater lake in Yunnan Province and the sixth largest in China. It covers an area of 30,000 Hectares and has an average depth of five meters. It is situated at the southern end of the city of Kunming which has a population of around seven million people.

In the summer of 2007, just like Lake Taihu, there was a massive algal bloom of Cyanobacteria, which had exactly the same effect on the surrounding area as happened in Wuxi and Len Harris was officially invited to attend Kunming between the 5th and 15th of October 2008 to discuss a solution for their problem.

### Factors Affecting the Solution as we understood them

Sewage from Kunming (both treated and untreated) appeared to be the main cause of the problem.

### Lake Dianchi Information

| | | |
|---|---|---|
| Total Area of lake | = | 30,000 Hectares |
| Approximate area of lake to be cleared near Kunming | = | 25,000 Hectares |
| Number of times it must be cleared each year | = | 2 |
| Total Area to be harvested each year | = | 50,000 Hectares |
| Average depth of water | = | 5 Meters |
| Algae         covering most of the lake in 2007 | = | Cyanobacteria |

Which created a Bad smell - stopped fishing - restricted movement across lake
        - polluted water supply - affected tourism.

| | | |
|---|---|---|
| Most Common water plant found in lake | = | Water Hyacinth |

## ▦ SOLUTION OVERVIEW

Our solution was almost identical to the one we proposed for Lake Taihu.

# Case Study Four - China – Lake Yangzong (near Kunming) - Arsenic Removal and Water Quality Restoration

NOTE. Much of the groundwork used in producing the design for Lake Taihu was also incorporated in our solution to solving Lake Yangzong's problems.

## The Problem

Lake Yangzong is situated in the Yunnan Province of China, 45 kilometers east of the city of Kunming. The lake is a popular tourist area and provides recreational opportunities for the citizens of Kunming. As recently as 2002, the lake was noted for the quality of its water which was considered clean enough to drink.

The lake has a catchment area of 192 sq. km. and covers an area of 31 sq.km. with an average depth of 19 metres.

In September 2008 the lake was officially considered unfit for drinking or for any water based activities, when the provincial government announced that it had found high levels of arsenic in its waters, caused by various businesses which operated in the Yangzong basin. The level of arsenic contamination was found to be 0.128 mg/l.

## Factors Affecting the Solution as we understood them

Action would be taken locally to stop further contamination.
Water hyacinth (W.H.) is known to remove heavy metals from water and a strain had been developed locally, with longer roots and fewer leaves, which was claimed to remove heavy metals at a higher rate than normal.
Any solution should incorporate the use of these locally developed W.H.'s and should deal with the safe disposal of the harvested plant (and hence the arsenic) once they had done their job.

## The KESPL Solution for Lake Yangzong in October 2008

## ▨ SOLUTION OBJECTIOVES

To - Work with the Province of Yunnan to remove arsenic from Lake Yangzong by means of the specially adapted Water Hyacinth (W.H.)
To - Create a secondary industry which uses the harvested W.H.
To - Find a safe disposal mechanism for the arsenic.

## SOLUTION OVERVIEW

NOTE. Capital costs include the design, management and transport costs to the site for each item specified in each Phase of the Project and all the figures are in US$.

### Project 1 Phase 1
Supply and deliver one harvester capable of harvesting 30 Hectares (1200 Tonnes) of W.H. per day

Capital cost to supply harvester            $1,553,000

Anticipated annual running costs            $762,000

### Project 1 Phase 2
Supply and deliver one pumping station capable of pumping 250 tonnes per hour over a distance of 5 km.

Capital Cost to supply pumping station       $1,172,000

Anticipated annual running costs            $960,000

### Project 1 Phase 3
Supply and deliver one Water Separation Plant capable of handling 1200 Tonnes of harvested W.H. per day. The residue will then be pressed into blocks and the water which has been extracted will be returned to the lake.

Capital cost of plant            $1,457,000

Anticipated annual running costs            $780,000

No allowance has been made for the purchase or lease of land for any of the facilities detailed in either Project and no allowance has been made for building a jetty or for maintenance workshops.

This plant would need to run for 24 hours each day and would require 4 operators to be on duty at all times.
240 tonnes of water would be recycled back into the lake each day and 960 tonnes of solids would be generated each day.

### Project 2 Phase 1
Fermentation and methane extraction plant (similar in concept to Lake Taihu).

Capital cost of plant            $8,494,000

Some of the methane extracted from this process will be used to supply power and steam for the proposed Fibre Board Processing Plant and the balance of the methane will be sold at market prices.

**Methodology**
We calculated that it would take 3 days to fill the first fermentation tank.

After a further 7 days methane would start to be produced at sufficient rate to power the Fibre Board Plant and at that time we would start to feed the Fibre Board Process Plant with W.H.

After 15 days we would fill the second fermentation tank. When the second tank produced sufficient methane we would empty the first fermentation tank passing the residue to the Fibre Board Plant.

This cycle would continue throughout the season.

Whilst one fermentation tank would be producing methane, the other fermentation tank would be emptying the residue and then filling with fresh water hyacinth.

**Project 2 Phase 2**
Supply and commission one Fibre Board Processing Plant, capable of producing at least 300 Tonnes per day.

Capital cost of plant                                     $19,000,000

**Methodology**
This plant would commence running 10 days after the start of harvesting W.H. and would continue to run for 10 days after the harvest had finished.

The remaining months of the year would be used to maintain all of the equipment.

NOTE. W.H. should continue to be grown and harvested in Lake Yangzong once the current problem had been solved as a precaution against future contamination. We also suggested that W.H.be planted in Dianchi Lake to assist in the control of algae in that lake as well.

In the future, the proposed Fibre Board Processing Plant could be expanded to include W.H. from Dianchi Lake.

Anticipated annual running costs for the entire project would be in the region of $4,500,000

It was anticipated that the sale of the excess methane gas would more than cover the above running costs and that the sale of the finished Fibre Board would be a complete profit for the owners.

## Short Description of Complete Process

| 1. | Water Hyacinth is planted in Lake Yangzong | |
|---|---|---|
| 2. | As plants mature they are harvested using purpose built harvesters | |
| 3. | Harvester unloads into pumping station | |
| 4. | Pumping station delivers water hyacinth to Water Separation Plant | |
| 5. | First fermentation tank is filled with water hyacinth from Water Separation Plant | |
| 6. | Harvest stops for 7 days | |
| 7. | Harvest starts feeding pumping station to water separation plant to Fibre Board Processing Plant | This complete cycle takes approximately 37 days. |
| 8. | After 15 days Water Separation Plant feeds second fermentation tank for 3 days | |
| 9. | Water Separation Plant returns to feeding Fibre Board Processing Plant | |
| 10. | After 7 days second fermentation tank is producing sufficient methane to run Fibre Board Processing Plant | |
| 11. | Methane to run Fibre Board Processing Plant is switched from first to second fermentation tank | |
| 12. | Residue from first fermentation tank is sent to Fibre Board Processing Plant progressively. | |
| 13. | After 15 days Water Separation Plant feeds first fermentation tank for 3 days | |
| 14. | This cycle is repeated for the duration of the season | |

# Case Study Five - Kununurra W.A. - Design a Trial Wetland Filter

### The Problem

Farm land in the Ord Irrigation Area Stage One, receives water from Lake Argyle, via Lake Kununurra and the irrigation canals and after watering the crops which have been planted, releases the water back into the Ord River.

It was discovered that certain pesticides used on the farms, in particular Atrazine, which was used on the maize and sugar cane crops was found to leave high concentrations in the water samples which were taken, particularly in the month of August, after the planting of the maize crop.

### Factors Affecting the Solution as we understood them

The client required a 'Free Surface Constructed' Wetland filter, which had to be a natural wetland using plant and biological controls.

The test site should cover approximately 5.5 Hectares and would receive input from about 550 hectares of farmland.

All the earth excavated was to be re-used on the site.

### The KESPL Solution for a Trial Wetland Filter 2010

## ▨ SOLUTION OVERVIEW

Excavate a channel 33 metres wide with varying depths.

The central part of the channel being 3 metres wide and 2 metres deep. Either side of the central channel is a secondary channel being 5 metres wide and one metre deep and either side of that channel is a third channel which is 10 metres wide and 0.5 metres deep.

A flood by-pass channel would also be dug which would be 3 metres wide and 3 metres deep.

The excavated earth would be used to construct high banks either side of the channel.

Planting Programme - Main Channel - Nothing.
      Secondary channel - Reed bed.
      Tertiary Channel - Cumbungi, Ribbon Weed etc.
      Banks -.Trees and bushes

Estimated 45,000 water plants plus 2,000 trees and bushes would be required.

The earth to be removed from every one metre of channel excavated would amount to 26 cubic metres.

## Wetlands Construction Kununurra
## Area = 370 Metres Long by 150 Wide

────── Baffles    Central Channel Runs for approx 650 metres.
Entry & Flood By-pass Channels Run for approx 530 metres.
Estmated 15,500 Cubic Metres of Earth to Move

## ▨ AREA OF COST FOR WETLAND PROJECT

NOTE. 1 Hectare = 10,000 Sq Metres so 5.5 Hectares = 55,000 Sq Metres.
All figures are in Australian Dollars.

| | | |
|---|---|---|
| Design & Consultancy | = | 16,000 |
| Site Costs @ $2 per Sq Metre | = | 110,000 |
| Baffles @ $150 per Metre | = | 45,000 |
| Sluice Gates @ $22,000 each | = | 88,000 |
| Plants/Planting @ 60 cents each | = | 27,000 |
| Trees & Bushes Planting@ $2 each | = | 4,000 |
| Contingency | = | 30,000 |
| | | |
| Total Estimated Cost of Project | = | $320,000 |

There was some talk of the need for an 'On Farm' poison filter which we believed would cost in the region of $50,000 per filter.

# Appendix

**▓ Contacts**

By email - To Lucidus Smith   info@lucidus-smith.co.uk


By mail    - To the Company Secretary,
             Lucidus Smith Ltd
             c/o Taylor Roberts CA
             15b Somerset House
             Hussar Court
             Waterlooville
             Hampshire
             PO7 7SG
             England



Website - http://lucidus-smith.co.uk/


To Annamarie Gervais
Jenson Technologies
412 Summer Mountain Dr.
San Marcos, TX 78666
512-393-5073
512-393-5074 (Fax)
www.lakemower.com
info@lakemower.com

# Abbreviations used in the book

| | |
|---|---|
| Acrolein | The poison used to kill the weeds in the Ord Irrigation canals. It is a severe pulmonary irritant and lachrymatory agent. |
| ANRL | Agro-Nutritional Research Laboratory |
| AVG | Aquatic Vegetation Groomer |
| CC | The Chemistry Centre |
| DEC | The Department of Environment and Conservation (Western Australia) |
| EPBC | The Environment Protection and Biodiversity Conservation Act 1999 |
| KESPL | Kimberley Environmental Solutions Pty Ltd |
| KDC | Kimberley Development Commission |
| k/h | Kilometres per hour |
| kms | Kilometres |
| KREAC | Kununurra Region Economic Aboriginal Corporation |
| MG People | The Miriuwung and Gajerrong People |
| NIMASA | Nigerian Maritime Administration and Safety Agency |
| NIR Testing | Near Infra Red Testing to determine the levels of moisture, protein, fat, starch, ash, fibre and energy in animal fodder. |
| OIC | Ord Irrigation Cooperative Ltd |
| OLWI | Ord Land and Water Inc. |
| ORIS | Ord River Irrigation Scheme |
| SWEK | The Shire of Wyndham and East Kimberley |
| W.A. | Western Australia |
| W.H. | Water Hyacinth |

# Water weeds found in Lake Kununurra and along the shore (list created 2007)

| LATIN NAME | COMMON NAME | ROOTED | FLOAT | LENGTH | WEED STATUS |
|---|---|---|---|---|---|
| Ceratopteris thalictroides | Water Sprite | | Yes | | ? |
| Chara | Muskgrass | | Yes | | ? |
| Eleocharis | Spikerush | Yes | | | High |
| Hydrilla verticillata | Hydrilla | Yes | | | V. High |
| Ipomoea diamantinensis | Water Spinach | Yes | | | V. High |
| Marsilea mutica | Nardoo | Yes | | | ? |
| Myriophyllum (many) | Milfoil | Yes | | 18 ins | V. High |
| Najas (many) | Water nymph | Yes | | | High |
| Nymphaea (many) | Water lily | Yes | | | Low |
| Nymphoides indica | Water lily | Yes | | | Low |
| Persicaria attenuata | Knotweed | Yes | | | ? |
| Phragmites australis | Common Reed | Yes | | | ? |
| Potamogeton tricarinatus | Pond weed | | Yes | 3ft | V. High |
| Tacca leontopetaloides | Bat Flowers | Yes | | | ? |
| Typha domingensis | Cumbungi | Yes | | 3ft | V. High |
| Urochloa mutica | Para grass | Yes | | 6ft | V. High |
| Utricularia gibba | Bladderwort | | Yes | | ? |
| Valisnaria Spiralis | Ribbon Weed | Yes | | 8ft | High |
| Wolffia angusta | Duck weed | | Yes | | Low |

| TREES FOUND IN VICINITY OF LAKE | COMMENTS |
|---|---|
| Melaleuca Viridiflora | Tea tree |
| Eucalyptus Microtheca | Essential oils |
| Eucalyptus Camaldulensis | Salt Tolerant |
| Nauclea Orientalis | |
| Indian Sandal-wood Plantations | |

# Equipment Designed/Built by KESPL

## The Weed Cutting Pontoon

### ▮ Technical Objective

1. To provide a lightweight covered cutting platform to be used primarily on the irrigation canals with two or three Jenson weed cutters.
2. To be able to be launched and handled by two people and to be propelled by a single outboard motor.
3. To be easily transported/stored with low maintenance costs.
4. To give sufficient protection from freshwater crocodiles and snakes.

The pontoon was constructed by a boat builder in Mandurah for a cost of around $15,000 and proved to be very successful on the canals where the flow of the water took the cut weed down to a net which was stretched across the canal. This picture shows the pontoon clearing weed in Lily Creek Lagoon.

The 35 Ton Capacity Harvester designed for the smaller Chinese lakes.

## Technical Objective

1. The harvester must be a self-contained system, self-powered and capable of operating on the water in rough and windy conditions.
2. It must be transportable over public roads.
3. It must be capable of cutting, loading and unloading both bottom rooted and floating aquatic plants and algae, without manual assistance.

(An artists impression.)

5 Metres wide and 15 metres long - Gross Weight = 25 Tonnes - Displacement = 75 Tonnes - Travelling at >3 kms. per hour for 20 hours a day and requiring a crew of three.

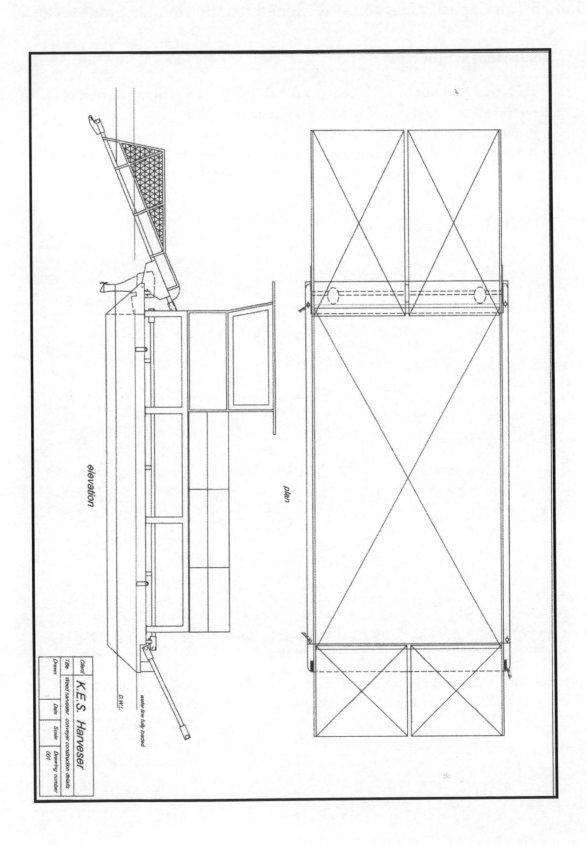

elevation

plan

D.W.L.

water line fully loaded

| Client | K.E.S. Harveser | | | |
|---|---|---|---|---|
| Title | Weed harvester  conveyer construction details | | | |
| Drawn | Date | Scale | Drawing number | |
| | | | 001 | |

The Conveyor for removing water weed from the canals.

## Technical Objective

1. To remove aquatic weed from the waterways with minimum manual assistance.
2. To be able to be set up and dismantled by two people.
3. To be easily transportable.

Designed, constructed shipped to Kununurra and tested by the shareholders in just under a month for a cost of $25,000. At a later stage an 'A' frame was used for the supporting legs which made it much more stable.

# KESPL Safe Work Instructions

## Setting up to Harvest Ribbon Weed from the Channels.

### Preparation

| Step | Description | Details | Contact | Done |
|------|-------------|---------|---------|------|
| | **2 weeks prior to Harvesting** | | | |
| 1 | Plan dates for harvesting with OIC | Ensure that OIC do not plan to dose channel with Acrolein during or immediately prior to planned harvest. | Manager<br><br><br>Assistant Manager | |
| 2 | Contact Countryman Hire to arrange labour and equipment for the week's harvest. Hiab and men arrive at equipment store at 8:00 am and semi arrives at KREAC at 10:00am | Requirements: 2 men familiar with the process, Hiab truck to pick up pontoon from store, flat bed semi-trailer and Merlo to pick conveyor from KREAC, Ute to pick other equipment from store. | Manager | |
| 3 | Contact KREAC to arrange use of truck and access to conveyor and drying area. | Drying area needs to be slashed a few days prior to laying Ribbon Weed on for drying. | Manager | |
| 4 | Contact Water Corporation to arrange to apply for Permit to Work when you arrive in town. Also plan for inductions for any person that will be working on the job. | Ensure that all persons that will be working on the job are inducted to work on Water Corporation assets. | Assistant Manager | |
| 5 | Arrange for batteries to be charged before arrival | Batteries are kept at the charging station in store | Manager | |
| 6 | Book accommodation. | Lakeview Apartments. | Receptionist | |
| 7 | Book hire vehicles | Thrifty car hire | Receptionist | |
| Step | **Description** | **Details** | **Contact** | **Done** |
| | 1 Week Prior to Harvesting | | | |
| 1 | Confirm all bookings as per above. | | | |
| | On arrival at Kununurra | | | |
| 1 | Pick up hire Ute at airport | Best option – dual cab Ute | Receptionist | |
| 2 | Book into accommodation | Unpack suitcases, shopping, | Receptionist | |
| 3 | Contact Water Corporation and pick up Clearance to Work Permit. | Follow format of last permit | Assistant Manager | |
| 4 | Pick up any items sent up by truck | Preferred transport company – Centurion Transport | | |
| | Setting up for Cutting Channels | | | |

| 1 | Pick up pontoon and other items from store | Hiab arrives at 8:00 am. Load pontoon and cover onto Hiab. Load batteries from charging station at rear of store. Pick up outboard, fuel tanks, cutters, generator, pump, nets, tools and black box from store adjacent to offices. | | |
|---|---|---|---|---|
| 2 | Place pontoon into water adjacent to the outlets north of Mills Rd bridge on M1 channel. | Unload all equipment at this point close to the bridge. | Team of 3 | |
| 3 | Fit the outboard onto the pontoon and put the net on the pontoon. | 2 men stay and fit the net from the north/west side under the bridge to the star picket located on the other side of the channel. | | |
| 4 | Pick up conveyor from KREAC yard. | Low Loader will arrive at KREAC at 10:00 am. Pick up using forklift. As the weight is taken remove the trestles from under and refit under frame but above chain when loading onto truck. Load with drive motor facing the front of the truck. | | |
| 5 | Unload conveyor at load out point. | Lift off truck (forklift). Place the conveyor as close as possible to final position on trestles. | | |
| 6 | Set up conveyor | Lift up to angle by fitting 4 leg chains at lifting points marked on cross bars with soft slings attached at lower end. As the Merlo takes the weight, unhook the brace legs and leave to hang. Position the conveyor so that the pickup point is under the water almost level with the top of the lower sprocket. Tighten all braces while the conveyor is still hooked to the Merlo. Fit the cross braces to the long support legs and tighten. Release the weight from the Merlo and check that the structure is sturdy. If structure is sturdy and strong, unhook the Merlo. Fit the take up wheel as high as possible and align with the centre of the conveyor. Check that there are no obstructions to the chain. Ensure that all personnel stand clear and connect conveyor to the generator and start/stop. If all seems good, start the conveyor and inspect that there are no rubbing or grating areas and that idle roller runs freely. Install barricade tape around legs of conveyor. All OK, run conveyor as needed. | | |

## Cutting the Ribbon Weed from the Channels

### Preparation

| Step | Description | Details | Contact | Done |
|---|---|---|---|---|
| 1 | Place pontoon into water adjacent to the outlets north of Mills Rd bridge on M1 channel. | | | |
| 2 | Fit the outboard onto the pontoon and put the net on the pontoon. | 2 men stay and fit the net from the north/west side under the bridge to the star picket located on the other side of the channel. | | |
| 3 | Lay the net from the tie point adjacent to the channel outlet on the north/east and run directly across the channel | Ensure that the net is not crossed over or tangled. Make sure that the net is tight enough that it doesn't get caught in the outlets. Fit extra floats under the top rope of the net evenly spaced across the channel. | | |
| 4 | Fit the cutters and cover to the pontoon. Ensure that all the grub screws are tight on the cutters before starting. | Secure the pontoon to shore close to the bridge and fit the cover first. Fit the centre cutter first so that the motor lays under the side cutter motors. Stagger the fitting of the side cutters so that the motors lay alongside each other when laid down for transport. | | |
| 5 | Cut the area between the net and the bridge. | As this is a reasonably small area it is best to cut back and forth across the channel. Ensure that all weed is cut in this area. | | |
| 6 | Remove the cover and drive the pontoon under the bridge to the other side | The cover needs to be removed to allow head room under the bridge. | | |
| 7 | Replace the cover and cut first 100 metres of channel. | This area needs to be cut clean as it is our base of operations. | | |
| 8 | Remove the cutters and cover and place on the south side of the bridge | Place the cutters and cover on the western side of the channel. | | |
| 9 | Take the east end of the net and drag with weed inside to the tie point through the bridge | A rope needs to be attached to the east end of the net and pulled tight along the desired route before the net is loosened from the original stake. This may need two men on the shore near the southern stake to ensure that the net does not get caught in the outlets by keeping it tight at all times. | | |
| 10 | Assist with setting up the conveyor if necessary. | | | |
| 11 | Move the pontoon back to the south side of the bridge and refit the cover and cutters as before. | Start cutting upstream in a southerly direction working from the east bank of the channel. To avoid getting tangled in cut weed it is best to cut upstream on the east side and downstream on the west side. | | |
| 12 | Pack up for the day. | Pack into the Ute: cutters, batteries, outboard, gaf, tarp, fuel tank, and any other small items. Two batteries will need to be charged overnight. The pontoon can be tied up under the Mills Rd bridge. | | |
| 13 | Resume cutting the next day. | Load up and set up the pontoon and continue cutting towards Ivanhoe Rd. This section usually takes about two days. Ensure that you have sufficient water and sunscreen and fuel for the outboard. | | |

| 14 | Move pontoon over Ivanhoe Rd | Book with Guerinonis to meet Hiab at Ivanhoe at 0700 in the morning of the day you want to relocate. Advise Jo the previous day. DO NOT LOAD OR UNLOAD PONTOON NEAR OVERHEAD POWER LINES. | |
|----|------|------|---|
| 15 | Complete cutting channel | Continue cutting channels up to the main pump station at Lake Kununurra. Book Hiab to pick up pontoon at expected completion time. | |
| 16 | Pick up pontoon and return to Rogers Machinery | Hiab arrives at 8:00 am. Load pontoon and cover onto Hiab. Leave batteries at charging station at rear of store's workshop. Pick up outboard, fuel tanks, cutters, generator, pump, nets, tools and black box and return to store adjacent to offices. | |

# Laboratory Fodder Analysis Results

29 March 2007

Kimberley Environmental Solutions

Results of the analysis of four feed samples as received on 16 March 2007.

| Analysis | 1. W2 Paragrass | 2. W3 Milfoil | 3. W5 Cumbungi | 4. W6 Ribbon Weeds |
|---|---|---|---|---|
| Crude Protein (%) N x 6.25 | 9.1 | 17.7 | 5.1 | 14.2 |
| Acid Detergent Fibre (%) | 46.5 | 31.0 | 52.1 | 35.1 |
| Digestibility (%) | 49.1 | 65.4 | 42.8 | 60.6 |
| Metabolisible Energy MJ/Kg | 6.3 | 9.1 | 5.3 | 8.3 |

Comments:

W2 Paragrass

Acid detergent value is high, resulting in low digestibility, however the crude protein level is good considering the type of plant material, which results in higher energy value than expected.

W3 Milfoil

Crude protein level is very good, acid detergent fibre value is moderately high, resulting in average to good digestibility and energy values.

W5 Cumbungi

Acid detergent fibre value is high, resulting in low digestibility, crude protein and metabolisible energy values are low, which may be expected of this type of plant material.

W 6 Ribbon Weeds

Acid detergent fibre is moderately high, and crude protein is at a good levels, digestibility and metabolisible energy values are average.

10 July 2007
**Ref: D 0586**

Kimberley Environmental Solutions

Results of the analysis of three weed samples as received on 20 June 2007.

| Analysis | Lily's | Cumbungi | Pond Weed |
|---|---|---|---|
| **Crude Protein (%), N x 6.25** | 10.4 | 11.5 | 11.2 |
| **Acid Detergent Fibre (%)** | 37.4 | 42.9 | 34.2 |
| **Digestibility (%)** | 57.1 | 53.1 | 60.1 |
| **Metabolisible Energy MJ/Kg** | 7.7 | 7.0 | 8.2 |

Comments:

The crude protein shows values which may be compared to values expected of oat grain. The acid detergent fibre values are fairly high, resulting in somewhat low digestibility values, and hence low to moderate metabolisible energy values, especially the Lily and Cumbungi samples, which contained high amounts of cellulose and silica matter.

From the three samples, the Pond Weed appeared to have the best nutritional status in terms of ruminants suitability.

# Application for Permit to Harvest Flora from Lily Creek Lagoon for Commercial Purposes

Sir/Madam,

Thank you for providing the format that we can use to apply for a clearing permit for our proposed operations in Lily Creek Lagoon.

*Specifics of the area proposed to be cleared:*

- *A map with the exact area outlined [include GPS co-ordinates of all boundaries]*

  A map detailing the area, complete with GPS co-ordinates of all boundaries is attached in a separate document.

- *Accurate, total area to be cleared in hectares.*

  The total area of Lily Creek Lagoon is 1.499sq km. KES intend to harvest 15 hectares, which equates to 10% of the lagoon area, at any one time. As the cut areas become re-established, the adjacent areas will be cut thus ensuring the sustainability of the project.

*Full project description:*

- *Details of the history of the site, including current land uses, historical clearing for what purpose, previous disturbance [fire, feral animals, human disturbance, weeds] and the extent of impacts.*

  Lily Creek Lagoon covered a much smaller area before the development of Lake Kununurra with the construction of the Ord Irrigation System (circa 1960). Previous to that time the area was covered with water only during the peak "wet season" period. Since the area has been designated a Ramsar Wetland of Significance, the level of water has been constantly maintained by Water Corporation of WA. The Shire of Wyndham East Kimberley (SWEK) has undertaken some mechanical control of Combungi (Typha Domingus) on the northern banks to improve the aesthetic outlook of the area. Over the last 10 years some tourism operators have used mechanical means to remove all flora from the boating channels.

  The mechanical control being carried out by SWEK has succeeded in stopping the encroachment of Combungi into the water way. In the areas where SWEK have not carried out any mechanical control, the Combungi has encroached into the water way, restricting access to banks and causing silt to build up under the plants and reducing the area of this body of water. In some areas Combungi has encroached into the water way by up to 70 meters.

The clearing of boating channels, carried out by tourism operators, has had limited success. The methods used involve removing the whole of the plants and may disturb the bed of the water ways.

Kimberley Environmental Solutions (KESPL) have cut sample areas of Lily Creek Lagoon measuring 1 meter square each month for the past 6 months. Samples of Ribbon Weed were cut at between 100mm and 150mm above the roots. Sample areas cut in January had re-grown to original height when checked in late May. The growth rate appeared uniform each month between January and May. Samples of Pond Weed were cut at between 100mm and 150mm above the roots. Sample areas cut in January had re-grown to 50% of original height when checked in late May. The growth rate appeared uniform each month between January and May. Samples of Combungi were cut at between 00mm and 50mm above the roots. Sample areas cut in January had re-grown to original height when checked in late March. The growth rate was extremely rapid and the sample area was indistinguishable from uncut plants after late March.

KESPL harvested an area of Lily Creek Lagoon adjacent to the end of Messmate Way measuring approximately 100 meters by 50 meters. Pond Weed and Lilies were cut at 100mm above the roots and all cut material was removed from the water. This harvesting was carried out between 26/05/07 and 29/05/07. When inspected on 2/07/07 vigorous re-growth had started and there was a marked difference in water clarity from the uncut areas. In the test area underwater visibility range was about 3 meters. In untreated areas the underwater visibility range was 0.5 meters. The test area surface showed no significant algae growth while the untreated area had algae growth covering the surface and about 40mm thick.

- *Specifics of how the clearing is to occur – manual/mechanical/chemical, time of year.*

KESPL will use mechanical means to cut the flora at between 100mm and 150mm above the roots and remove it from the water. This method avoids disturbing the beds of the water way and eliminates the possibility of erosion. It also encourages rapid re-growth which inhibits algae growth and improves water clarity.

Where floating areas of Combungi occur, KESPL will remove the entire plants to within 3 meters of the shoreline.

In order to provide sanctuaries for fauna, KESPL intends to cut in a patchwork pattern. This involves cutting an area 100 meters by 100 meters and leaving an area of similar size adjacent to it on either side. Once the cut areas have re-established themselves, we will return and cut the areas previously uncut. From our observations, cut areas should re-establish themselves in about 5 months but this time span may increase depending on seasonal influences. In this manner we expect to cut the 20%

of the area of Lily Creek Lagoon once per year starting in March and finishing in December.

- *Specifics of what the land is intended to be used for.*
  At present the lake is used as an access way for tourism boats and recreational fishing boat launching. However the density of weed growth has severely restricted its use in recent years. The natural beauty of the area will be retained using our method of flora control.

- *Details of offsets – areas of vegetation proposed to be retained and for what reasons [unsuitability of some areas for proposed use due to soil types, high erosion]*

In order to provide sanctuaries for fauna, KESPL intends to cut in a patchwork pattern. This involves cutting an area 100 meters by 100 meters and leaving an area of similar size adjacent to it on either side. Once the cut areas have re-established themselves, we will return and cut the areas previously uncut.

- *Details of any rehabilitation that is proposed.*

From our observations 100% re-growth occurs in approximately 5 months. KESPL commit to monitor, and report to DEC, the re-growth of cut areas at regular intervals. As the cut flora will become an asset to KESPL, it is in our own interest to ensure that the biodiversity of the area remains stable.

- *Site photos* NOTE. Recent photographs are attached in separate document.

<u>Address the ten principles (form attached) with emphasis on plants and animals present within the site and surrounding the site.</u>

- *If the clearing looks like it will cause environmental harm against any of the principles, what measures are you going to take to reduce the harm? Your commitments here may enable the permit to be granted.*

The ten principles have been addressed in a separate attachment.

<u>Lease details and Lessor consent:</u>

- *Copy of lease [or license] agreement proving entitlement to area proposed to be cleared.*

KESPL has been granted a "License for Scientific or Other Purposes No SL????" for this area.

Environment Australia has classed this action as a "Prescribed Action" and WH Projects (an associated company with KESPL) are described as the "Sole Proponents of said action". Copies of these documents are available on request.

- *Shire*

SWEK is supportive of the work being carried out by KESPL as part of a feasibility study. KESPL has written to the shire and asked for written authority to broaden the scope of their approval.

- *Department of Water*

The Department of Water is aware of the work being carried out by KESPL under our "License for Scientific or Other Purposes No SL????" for this area. We have been informed by the department that they will not issue a license or lease until such time as DEC approve this action. We therefore ask that this item be held in abeyance until a decision is made by DEC to approve or reject this application. If this application is approved, the department has suggested that they would have no objection to granting a license or lease.

<u>Land owner approval:</u>

- *Shire*

SWEK is supportive of the work being carried out by KESPL as part of a feasibility study. KESPL has written to the shire and asked for written authority to broaden the scope of their approval.

- *Department of Water*

The Department of Water is aware of the work being carried out by KESPL under our "License for Scientific or Other Purposes No SL????" for this area. We have been informed by the department that they will not issue a license or lease until such time as DEC approve this action. We therefore ask that this item be held in abeyance until a decision is made by DEC to approve or reject this application. If this application is approved, the department has suggested that they would have no objection to granting a license or lease.

- *Department for Planning and Infrastructure*

The Department for Planning and Infrastructure is aware of the work being carried out by KESPL under our "License for Scientific or Other Purposes No SL????" for this area. We have been informed by the department that they will not issue a license or lease until such time as DEC approve this action. We therefore ask that this item be held in abeyance until a decision is made by DEC to approve or reject this application. If this application is approved, the department has suggested that they would have no objection to granting a license or lease.

*Endorsements and other approvals you still require or have applied for [include documentation]:*

- *Bed and Banks permit (Department of Water)*

  The Department of Water will not issue a Beds and Banks Permit until such time as the DEC approves this application.

- *Planning approval (Shire)*

  KESPL has been and will continue to work closely with SWEK in this matter. However the shire cannot issue Planning approval until DEC approves this application.

- *Environmental Protection Authority assessments or decisions*

  Environment Australia has endorsed this action as "a controlled action" and KESPL (through WH Projects) are nominated as the "Sole Proponents".

- *Native Title (Kimberley Land Council)*

  Kimberley Land Council have endorsed this proposal and provided us with a Letter of Support.

- *Sites of Aboriginal Significance (Department of Indigenous Affairs)*

  KES have been working closely with MG Corp in an attempt to identify the Traditional Owners of the area. We will contact the Department of Indigenous Affairs in the next few weeks to clarify the situation.

Yours sincerely,

Len Harris
Managing Director
Kimberley Environmental Solutions Pty Ltd

# Job Specifications for the Management Team running the Lake Taihu Project

## The Board of Directors

All directors must be able to speak and understand English.

### Chief Executive
Full Time - Reports to the Shareholders
Qualifications
Degree or Recognized Business Qualification in a related discipline.

Experience Required:
Minimum of twenty years experience in a related discipline with at least ten years experience in a senior management position.

Responsibilities:
Line Manager for the Managing Director, Plans & IT Director and Government Liaison Director.
Line Manager for the Executive Secretaries.
Chairman of the Board of Directors
Responsible to the shareholders for the efficient and profitable running of the company.

### Managing Director
Full Time – Reports to the CEO
Qualifications
Degree or Recognized Business Qualification in a related discipline.

Experience Required:
Minimum of fifteen years experience in Business with at least five years experience in a senior management position.

Responsibilities:
Line Manager for the Finance, Personnel and Operations Directors.
Line Manager for the Security Manager.
Public Relations and Media Announcements.
Responsibility for the hand-over of all completed projects from KESPL.
Responsibility for managing the day to day activities of the company.

**Planning and Information Technology Director**
Full Time – Reports to the CEO
Qualifications
Degree or Recognized Business Qualification in a related industry.

Experience Required:
Minimum of twenty years experience in the IT industry with at least ten years experience in a senior management position.
Minimum of ten years experience in a senior Planning Role

Responsibilities
Line Manager for the Planning and IT Manager.
To be responsible for all aspects of IT within the company.
To be responsible for all aspects of Planning & Control.
Purchasing sign off.
Contract Negotiation

**Finance Director**
Full Time - Reports to the MD
Qualifications
Degree or Recognized Business Qualification in Banking or Finance or Accounting.

Experience Required:
Minimum of fifteen years experience in Finance with at least five years experience in a senior management position.

Responsibilities
Line Manager for the Accounts Manager, Admin Manager and the Property Manager

Responsibility for all Finance, Salary, Administration, Property and Purchasing matters.

**Personnel Director**
Part Time – Reports to the MD
Qualifications
Degree or Recognized Business Qualification in Personnel or Law

Experience Required:
Minimum of fifteen years experience in Personnel or Law with at least five years experience in a senior management position.

Responsibilities
Line Manager for the Personnel Manager and for all Personnel and Legal Liaison matters.

## Operations Director
Full Time – Reports to the MD
Qualifications
Degree or Recognized Engineering Qualification.

Experience Required:
Minimum of fifteen years experience in Engineering with at least five years experience in a senior management position.

Responsibilities
Line Manager for the Production, Maintenance and Fleet Managers.
Responsibility for all Operational matters.

The Management Team
All Managers must be able to speak and understand English.

## Fleet Manager
Full Time - Reports to the Operations Director
Qualifications
Skippers Ticket.

Experience Required:
Minimum of twenty years experience as a captain of a boat with at least five years experience on a similar sized craft to the largest in the fleet.

Responsibilities
Line Manager for all senior captains.
Responsibility for all Fleet matters.
Must be able to skipper one of the principle ships in the Fleet.
Would normally attend Board Meetings

## Production Manager
Full Time - Reports to the Operations Director
Qualifications
Degree or Qualification in a related industry.

Experience Required:
Minimum of fifteen years experience in related field with at least five years experience in a management position.

Responsibilities
Line Manager for all senior Production staff.
Responsibility for all non Fleet production matters.

## Maintenance Manager

Full Time - Reports to the Operations Director
Qualifications
Degree or Qualification in a related industry.

Experience Required:
Minimum of ten years experience in related field with at least two years experience in a management position.

Responsibilities
Line Manager for all senior Maintenance staff.
Responsibility for all maintenance matters.

## Personnel Manager

Full Time - Reports to the Personnel Director
Qualifications
Degree or Qualification in Personnel

Experience Required:
Minimum of ten years experience in related field with at least three years experience in a management position.

Responsibilities
Line Manager for all Training and Personnel staff.
Wages and Salary planning and implementation.
Responsibility for all Contract Staff relationships.
Compliance with all Government regulations.

## Accounting Manager

Full Time - Reports to the Finance Director
Qualifications
Accountancy Degree or Qualification

Experience Required:
Minimum of twelve years experience since qualification with at least three years experience in a management position.

Responsibilities
Line Manager for all Accounting and Wages staff.
Responsibility for the preparation of Monthly/Quarterly/Annual accounts.
Compliance with all Government reporting requirements.
Liaison with company auditors.

## Admin Manager

Full Time - Reports to the Finance Director
Qualifications
Business Degree or Qualification

Experience Required:
Minimum of eight years experience with at least three years experience in a management position.

Responsibilities
Line Manager for all Admin and Reception staff.
Responsibility for non production/maintenance/accounting administration matters.

## I.T. Manager

Full Time - Reports to the Planning & IT Director
Qualifications Degree or Business Qualification in a related industry.

Experience Required:
Minimum of twelve years experience in related fields with at least two years experience in a management position.

Responsibilities
Line Manager for the I.T. professionals.
Design and Implementation of the I.T. strategy for China
All data and I.T. security matters
All software selection/implementation and training

## Planning and Property Manager

Full Time - Reports to the Planning/IT Director.

Experience Required:
Minimum of five years experience in the Planning/Legal/Property/Office arena.
At least two years Management experience.
Good communication skills.

Responsibilities
Line Manager for the Planning & Property professionals.
Man Manager for the IT professionals.
Creation of the Company Five Year/Two Year and Annual Operating Plans.
All Property/Facilities Management and related matters within the company including the Selection/Control/Liaison with the Cleaning and Gardening contractors.

**Security Manager**
Full Time - Reports to the Managing Director.

Experience Required:
Minimum of fifteen years experience in a related field with at least five years experience in a senior security position.

Responsibilities
Line Manager for the security professional
All security related matters within the company
Selection/Control/Liaison with the Security Guard company.

# About the Directors of KESPL

**Len Harris** (Chairman and CEO)

He started East Kimberley Engineering Pty Ltd in 1980 and built it up to a permanent workforce of forty personnel in varying trades over a period of 12 years.

Most recently, Len was engaged as a Construction Coordinator for Alcoa at their Pinjarra/Wagerup sites south of Perth. Len lives in WA.

**Neil Woollacott** (Managing Director)

He completed a Bachelor of Engineering (Civil) Degree from UWA in 1979, and after working for seven years as an engineer, entered the field of Real Estate.

He has had extensive experience in business ownership and management.

Neil has been the chairman of the board of the Small Business Centre in the Peel Region (Honorary capacity). Neil lives in WA

**Michael Bray** (Finance Director)

He was a Fellow of the Certified Practicing Accountant's Society since 1981, but has now sadly passed away.

He ran his own accountancy practice for 24 years and was a director of a number of companies, in advisory and accountancy roles.

**Alan Smith** (Director)

He is a retired Company Secretary who previously worked for Lexmark International Ltd and who resides in the UK but spends his winters in Australia. He has a broad range of experience in I.T., corporate law and business management principles and is currently trying his hand as an author (under the pen name of Lucidus Smith).

# A Guide to a Waterways Management Plan

# Contents

# INTRODUCTION and OBJECTIVES

## ▨ INTRODUCTION

For Waterways Management to be effective, those involved must understand the needs and include all of the interested parties in the form of an Advisory Group.

This group should also include all of the necessary professional/technical/environmental experts required for each of the different aspects of the Waterways and the lands adjoining them.

Even a basic Waterways Management Plan is better than no plan at all.

The ideas contained in this Guide will enable you to make a start at developing a plan that is right for you and which you can develop into something more specific to meet your needs, with regard to the time available to you and the budget that has been allocated for the task.

As a growing world population seeks to use our waterways more and more, for both recreational and business purposes, there is an urgent need for those responsible to plan for their maintenance and improvement.

Along with the requirement for us to better understand the various negative impacts to our waterways that will result from these increased activities, we need to understand the options available to us in order to plan for the control of these aforementioned impacts.

## ▨ OBJECTIVES of PLAN

To document and understand the waterways and adjoining land, along with the flora and fauna which exist there.

To protect the waterways and adjoining land from damage and erosion and to safeguard and improve the water quality along with the flora and fauna found there.

To maintain the waterways in good condition in order to meet the various uses which has been agreed for them.

A Waterways Management Plan can be used to encourage good relations with all of the interested parties and to identify their concerns, requirements and contributions towards maintaining and improving the various facilities associated with the waterways.

It should have realistic objectives and set goals which have been agreed as reasonable and attainable in a sensible timeframe and within the budget allocated.

# THE PLAN PROCESS

## 1. TIMEFRAMES

In planning terms, a five year period would be the normal start position for a plan, however, where tree planting and major civil engineering work is involved, it may be necessary to have a ten or fifteen year 'Overview Plan' in place as well.

A five year plan is normally considered long enough to achieve most goals and should be on a 'Top Down' approach.

For example:

By year five, the river will be two feet deeper, all obstructions will be removed, the banks will be strengthened and the two foot bridges will have been replaced and the footpath will have been renovated.

The tree planting in Smith's Wood, will have been completed and thinned out and the existing pathways altered to avoid sensitive habitats.

Two bird hides will be in place and the car park moved to the far side of the new building.

Water quality and flow rate will be maintained and monitoring stations installed at three points along the river.

Etc. etc.

We then come to the Two Year Plan which will specifically set out the different projects that will actually be undertaken in this timeframe along with the expected costs, personnel and disruptions involved.

Lastly we come to the One Year Plan which will detail the various projects that will start in the next twelve months, along with all the resources that will be required to support them and the timeframe that each requires, along with the dependency that they have on each other and the disruption they will cause.

For example:

Project Title - Construct a new Path in Smith's Wood.

Manpower - Surveyor - Chainsaw operator - Building contractor.
Cost Estimate - £7,500 to £8,500

Timeframe - during the period March 1st to September 30th - for thirty seven days.
Dependency - Council to have finished the road extension and to have constructed the new fence with wooden access gate.

Disruptions - No public access to the wood while the work is in progress.

## 2. PRIORITIES

List the concerns of the Interested Parties and of the Technical/Environmental experts.

For example:
Footbridge damaged and dangerous.
Swans being stoned by drunken youths.
Walkers in wood disturbing Barn Owls.
River flow affected by weed growth.
Exotic Species of plant and fish to be removed.

List the requirements of the Interested Parties and of the Technical/Environmental experts.

For example:

New fishing platform required by the angling club.
Bird hide required by ornithologists in Smith's Wood.
Three new moorings required by boating fraternity.
Need for speed limit on river to be enforced by residents committee.

Each item on the list should then be assessed for practicality, cost and support by everyone and then prioritised. (There may need to be some sort of weighting as to who can veto/support what.)

## 3. GOALS STATEMENT

These are general statements outlining what the group has agreed and hopes to achieve over the next five years. (See Timeframes above - Five Year Plan).

These could be made available to the media and open to public inspection.

A goals statement should also establish specific short- and long-term goals relating to the desired water quality of the waterway.

## 4. DETAILED OBJECTIVES FOR THE NEXT TWO YEARS

These are the detailed projects which the group has agreed to start during the next twenty four months. (See Timeframes above - One and Two Year Plan).

## 5. AUTHORISE ACTIONS

These are the detailed steps that need to be taken, in order to accomplish the objectives, in the order that has been stated.

For example:

The following items might appear on an Action List:

1. Woodland management.
Clear all rubbish from Smith's Wood.

2. Habitat protection
Re-route footpath away from swan nesting site.

3. Species introduction
Commence discussions with the Environmental Officer at Oldplace regarding the re-introduction of Newts.

4. Speed limit and wash
Replace all signs and liaise with River Police over speed boat nuisance.

5. Public Understanding/Awareness
Discuss a series of weekly items/pictures with the editor of the local newspaper.

6. Geological Survey
Survey both banks for soil type and underlying rock.

# DATA COLLECTION

The more you know and understand about your Waterways and the adjoining land, the better you can create and implement your plan.

A lot of the following information you may already have to hand, but it should be kept up to date and available to the Planning Team.

## 1. LOCATION/MAP

The map or maps, should cover the entire area you have responsibility for and should contain useful information regarding other waterways, estates, towns and villages and other sites that could affect you.

## 2. SIZE of AREA and WATERWAYS DIMENSIONS

Know how many hectares you cover and the length, breadth and depth of your waterways.

## 3. OWNERSHIP

You should know who owns the land you are responsible for as well as the land that joins your land and could affect your waterways. Which Councils and Utilities have responsibility for the roads, bridges, pylons etc. on or near your Waterways.

## 4. SITE DETAILS.

Types of Soil and Rock present, height above sea level, details of heights and slopes of nearby hills that might affect you.

The woodlands - size - flora and fauna - history.
Open land- size - flora and fauna - history.
Lakes, rivers, canals, ditches - water quality - hydrology - rainfall - pollutants - history - seasonal variations - flora and fauna.
Roads, paths, buildings, bridges, moorings, jetties and other structures.
Special Interest items.
Regular site activities - spraying - fertilising - thinning - cutting - harvesting
Regular site events - carnivals - visitors - Open Days - regattas

## 5. ACCESS

Document all of the roads, bridleways and paths that cross or come near to your boundaries.

## 6. SURROUNDING LAND USE

Farming, forestry, heathland, lakes, airports, government facilities, mining/gravel pits, industry etc.

## 7. ACTIVITIES LIKELY to CAUSE DAMAGE and NEEDING EXTREME CARE.

### Type of Activity:

Certain farming activities i.e. ploughing and mowing

The introduction of deer or other grazing animals.

The application of manure, fertilisers and lime.

The application of pesticides, including herbicides (weedkillers).

Dumping, spreading or discharge of any materials.

Lighting fires.

The release of any exotic animal, bird fish, plant or seed.

The killing or removal of any flora or fauna.

Infilling of ditches, drains, ponds, pools, marshes or pits.

Un-authorised recreational activities.

# THE PLANNING TEAM

I am not quite sure who said, "Please preserve us from well intentioned amateurs" maybe it was me, but everyone I know who has ever had to work with amateurs in a business environment, seems to have come to the same conclusion as myself.

In view of the above, I would advise that any 'Advisory Group' or 'Interested Parties' committee that needs to be included in the Planning Team, must be carefully chosen and their level of control and decision making ability, clearly defined and agreed, right at the very start.

## 1. ADVISORY GROUP MEMBERS

Identify all the groups who have a genuine and on-going interest in the good management of the Waterways.

Write a brief Job Description of the skills, experience and level of authority that each representative should bring. (Someone who cannot understand what is being discussed or is afraid to make decisions or is forever on the telephone checking things out with someone else, is the wrong person.)

Clearly state the time commitment that is expected from each group member and any expenses which you are prepared to reimburse.

Personal experience in your own locality will guide you as to whether you should invite any Council/Government representatives to join the Group, or whether you should just keep them informed..

## 2. THE TECHNICAL COMMITTEE

These members should have the relevant expertise to cover all the technical issues involved in Managing Waterways. They will probably come from your own staff group or are already involved in advising you on technical matters.

They will probably cover matters such as-

Water quality and hydrology.
Fish stocks and water plants.
Forestry and land management.
Wildlife and the environment.
Civil engineering.
Security.
Recreation and leisure.

It is essential that you nominate one person with the skill and experience of 'Chairing Meetings', to be your Chairman. You will also need to appoint another person with relevant skills, as your Meeting Secretary, to record the decisions that are made and to produce timely Minutes of the meetings.

## 3. POINTERS for a SUCCESSFUL PLANNING TEAM

Give careful thought to the Agenda and then stick to it at the meeting.
Do not apportion blame unless really un-avoidable.
All members should treat each other with respect and the Chairman should make sure that everyone is heard.
Aim for the consensus of all interested parties, but vote on it, if you have to.
Go out and inspect the Waterways and see the problems being discussed first hand.
Do not set out to change the world or its opinions, but stay focussed on what you can achieve.
Celebrate success and appreciate the contributions of all

## 4. TEAM EDUCATION

Get each member of the Advisory Group to give a ten minute overview of what their Group is about and what they hope to achieve.

Get each of the Technical Experts to give a twenty minute overview of their particular expertise, as it affects the waterways.

Go over any historical, geographical or geological aspects which the experts have not covered and review the data that has been collected for the site.

Inform the team of any 'Industry' concerns or problems or successes which may be relevant for the site.

Education should be ongoing, although you may need more in-depth sessions at the beginning and whenever members are replaced.

# PLAN IMPLEMENTATION AND CONTROL

## ▨ 1. OVERVIEW

Using the 'Action List' produced in The Plan Process phase, review each action in turn and list the individual tasks, manpower, costs, dependencies and complexities that comprise each action on the list.

Create a Critical Path Analysis of the Action List and review the findings with the Planning Team.

Once the final list has been agreed, appoint a Task Manager (Project Leader) for each of the initial concurrent tasks and get started.

Review progress on a weekly/monthly basis to start with and adjust the regularity of the reviews as experience dictates.

You should also have some form of 'Control' person in place, who is outside of the normal business of managing the Waterways and is not directly accountable to any of the Task Managers.

## ▨ 2. TASK DOCUMENTATION

These documents should include a statement regarding the problem being addressed, as well as the work which needs to be undertaken to solve the problem. There should be a central copy of all documents, written to an agreed format.

Trying to pick up a task from someone who is ill or has left suddenly is never an easy thing, but to discover they were keeping all the information in their head, creates a nightmare scenario.

For Example:

Task 1 Remove Rowan Trees. Project 1 - New Path in Smith's Wood.

The wood is primarily elm and other broad leaf trees and the Rowan trees are not naturally found in the wood and should be removed before they become a real nuisance and before any work on the path is started.

The head forester will mark all trees for felling during the first week of March and identify the sites where the logs are to be stacked. Some will be used to form wildlife habitats and others as posts in the River Bank Erosion Project.

The contractor will visit the site during the second and third week of March and fell the trees and cut them into logs and stack them in the specified sites. The contractor will remove 25% of logs for own use. All small branches and debris is to be shredded and heaped separately for future use and tree stumps treated to prevent further growth.

Manpower      - Head forester and his assistant for two days each.
              - Contractor - Brown Bros. Ltd for six man days in total.

Costs         - Contractor - £1,200.

Dependencies  - Weather conditions - Council bridge repairs not taking place.

Complexities  - May need to remove and re-site some bird boxes, need to keep      visitors out of the wood while work in progress.

Task Manager  - Head forester

Review        - Monthly starting end of March

For Example:

Task 3 Stabilise River Banks between Bridges. Project 2. Monitor and Stabilise River Banks.

The river banks between the two bridges have been identified as needing urgent attention due to natural erosion and the wash of speed boats not keeping to the limits.

The Waterways engineer will mark the positions where the supporting logs are to be sunk along the bank during the second week of April. He will inform the head forester of the number and size of logs required.

The contractor will visit the site during the remainder of April and will bring the necessary equipment to sink the logs and make them firm. They will then use willow hurdles to support the bank in the normal manner, backfilling where necessary.

Manpower      - Waterways engineer one day initially and half a day a week thereafter for the remainder of the task.
              - Head forester half a day.
              - Contractor - Jones Bros. Ltd for eight man days in total.

Costs         - Contractor - £1,500.
              - Equipment Hire - £1,000.

Dependencies  - Logs available from Smith's Wood Project

Complexities  - River users will need to be kept away from workmen and the fishing club must be kept informed of the work schedule.

Task Manager - Waterways engineer.

Review          - Weekly

## 3. ACCOUNTABILITY

A task manager who does not feel accountable for the task he or she is in charge of, will never finish on time and within budget.

An excuse for failure is always just that, 'an excuse'.

There has to be a formal 'sign off' process, with regular reviews and rewards for success and consequences for failure.

## 4. THE PLAN CONTROLLER

The Plan Controller is outside of the Review Process and in a large business, might well be part of an Internal Audit group. In essence it is an individual who can look at any task or project, completed, on-going or planned for the future and demand to be told exactly what is happening, where, why and at what cost.

The Plan Controller should report directly to the Chief Executive Officer (C.E.O.) and needs to be an individual of wide experience who is well respected within the organisation.

For some reason, Task Managers who dig large holes which they then fall into, seem inclined to keep on digging holes for themselves, rather than to call for help and admit something has gone wrong.

The Plan Controller's job, is to spot these holes in their early stages and act promptly to prevent them getting bigger or spreading to other areas.

## 5. DAY TO DAY BUSINESS.

Within the Plan there needs to be a clear understanding of the day to day business that needs to be carried out and which may need to take precedence sometimes, over the various Projects which are underway. These may include some, or all of the following:

Water quality monitoring and assessment.
Measuring the chemical, biological and physical composition of the water is essential to understanding how the waterway works and to identifying appropriate projects for the future.

Fish Stocks and Aquatic Vegetation monitoring and assessment.

Different fish and plants require different conditions to prosper, so changes here may well indicate unexpected changes in the waterways.

If the sport of fishing is a vital part of your economy, then the best way to protect and improve fish populations is to protect and improve fish habitats and water quality.

Aquatic vegetation is a natural part of most waterways and provides many benefits to fish, wildlife and people. They are one of the primary producers in the aquatic food chain, converting the basic chemical nutrients in the water and soil into plant matter that becomes food for other aquatic and terrestrial life.

Aquatic plants can improve water quality, protect river banks and the shores of lakes and improve the overall biodiversity of the waterway.

While aquatic vegetation performs these important functions, it can also interfere with the various different users of the waterway, if its growth is excessive.

Control of aquatic vegetation is appropriate when reasonable access to, and the use of the water is impeded. Control may be in the form of harvesting any excess vegetation and planting new areas, where required.

A list of noxious weeds should be produced and removal plans should be in place.


Wildlife monitoring and assessment

Changes to the wildlife may indicate changes in the environment or to other areas in your locality, which may affect you and which you may not have been informed about.

The different habitats should be documented and understood and regular inspections carried out to make sure they are being properly managed and protected.

Wildlife corridors should be discussed with adjacent land owners and then be built and maintained as required.

Exotic Species monitoring and control

An "exotic species" is a plant or animal not native to your waterway or the adjoining land.

Many of these have been introduced intentionally, but many more have escaped from farms, zoos, parks and gardens. Others have arrived on motor vehicles, boats, trailers, birds and mammals.

The introduction of any Exotic Species whether accidentally or intentionally from one habit to another is a risky business (Cane Toads in Australia).

With no predators, parasites, pathogens and competitors that keep their numbers in check, species introduced into new habitats often overrun their new home and crowd out native species. Once established, exotics are rarely eliminated.

Public Water Access

If you allow the public to access the waterways from your site, or to use your moorings and then to use the waterways for recreational purposes, you must make certain that your facilities are maintained in good condition and that you abide by all the local bye-laws which relate to your site.

# CONCLUSION

As more and more people seek to use our waterways, the risk of damage and pollution will continue to grow, as will the need to manage them properly and efficiently, so that future generations can continue to enjoy them in the same way that we have done.

Waterways Management will undoubtedly become more complex, as legislation grows and the demands placed upon our waterways becomes more diverse.

Planning need not be onerous, but it must be thorough and proper resources must be allocated to the Plan, to make certain that the specified tasks are completed and the required changes implemented.

As I said in the Introduction 'Even a basic Waterways Management Plan is better than no plan at all' and I hope the guidelines contained in this document will assist you with that task.

Lucidus Smith
23rd July 2014